To Babel and Back

To Babel and Back
Robert Minhinnick

seren

Seren is the book imprint of
Poetry Wales Press Ltd
Nolton Street, Bridgend, CF31 3AE
www.seren-books.com

ISBN 1-85411-401-8

The publisher works with the support of the Welsh Books Council

Printed in Plantin by CPD (Wales), Ebbw Vale

Cover image: Eamon Bourke

Contents

The Yellow Dust

MOST EVENINGS WE SIT on the porch and feel the air cool, watch darkness fall. And every evening the lightning offers its spectacle, bursting over the western horizon, ghosting into the north. Sometimes the hills carry an afterglow as if some tremendous furnace burns behind their slopes. Sometimes all we see are talons of electricity printed on the sky, vanishing in a moment.

Tonight we sip the steely Sedona beer from a collection of plastic beakers. Inside, Daniel throws out advice as to the progress of the meal. Yes, he has trimmed the skin from the garlic cloves. Yes, wearing plastic gloves, he has diced and rediced the chilis, the *jalapeños* lustreless and empurpled, the fierce scotch bonnets.

Amigos, he calls, you should try this.

This, apparently, is dangerous work. But we are forbidden entry to the kitchen where Daniel works alone, chopping chilis as close as the big-shouldered kitchen knife will allow.

So we sit and face the Mingus Mountains, counting between lightning flash and thunder roll, watching the Grand Ams pull up at the Moose Lodge across the way, Old Glory in ribbons above the parkade, while all the time on the pavement outside the porch, the kids are laughing in Spanish, naked in the dusk.

There hasn't been a breath of wind all day. The candle flames stand erect in the stillness. Lying back in our chairs, we aren't bothered by much at all. The morning's 7am expedition had seen to that. We had driven a mile up the road past Mescal Gulch and started walking north and east. There was a wetland ringed by bullrushes that soaked us to the knees, but soon we were climbing. We passed a wooden cage where cowbirds were snared. Their whispering pursued us as far as the first junipers, and into an aromatic country, its scree rattling underfoot. Since arriving I had been troubled by a raw throat. Blame the dust and the parched air, people said, and they would bring me sprigs of mesquite. Breathe it in, they urged, and I would carry garlands to Wal Mart and Kaktus Kate's, holding the leaves to my nose, inhaling their oily physic.

Now, every other trace of greenery was mesquite, wind-twisted and hunched against the hillside. I broke the leaves, rubbed silver juniper berries to a paste. The air was a pharmacy, and as we climbed, the sun rose, rowelling our backs, stones big and small scittering out of our footsteps to where we had laboured only moments before.

And then we were on the crest of the mesa, tapping with our snakesticks through the brush. It was easy to think, despite the odd strand of barbed wire, the occasional tin can, maybe twenty or thirty years old and preserved by the aridity, that few had walked where we walked since the Yavapai had commanded the heights. Before them a nameless race had flourished. The Spanish, who discovered traces of their civilisation, christened them 'Sanagua': the people who lived without water. From high we could see a ruin called Tuzigoot, a place they had occupied. All this had been their country. And then they had vanished, leaving empty kivas and melon seeds, a tantalising pottery smeared with ochre, dry as ash. And now we stood on their land, brazen, hatless, posing for photographs on the Sanaguan summit, searching for the arroyo track down the other side of the slope.

Daniel handed round our pemmican: tough strips of celery. Essential for expeditionaries, he said. It was full of fluids that leaked slowly into the gut. Below, jays crackled in the *manzanilla* as we slithered into the wash, its red rocks worn smooth by torrents that now were inconceivable. Waters had eroded the sandstone walls of the canyon, yet water was the element that no longer existed in that world. There was shelter in the dark spaces beneath the cliffs, but Daniel's tales of three hundred pound iguanas drove us on. We sucked an Evian bottle, skirted the sentinels of *ocotillo*, and walked.

The trick with guacamole, calls the cook from the kitchen, is to leave the pit in the fruit when you mash up the avocados. That way it doesn't go brown. Stays a nice pale green.

Like the lightning, someone says. And I can smell the *cilantro* as Daniel stirs it into the salsa, the fragrance growing like the darkness. Mexican parsley, they call the herb hereabouts, heraldic leaves and a cookpot-filling stink.

Now the kids are beside us, taking scorpions and chafers out of matchboxes. One has found a dead cricket bigger than his hand. He holds it for display and we look into its mountain lion face. Behind the wash-house, the cicadas abrade the night, their racket too loud for life, a madness in its surround-sound circuitry.

Hey, but it's hot, hot, hot, Daniel is calling.

You can't be ready for this.

He pauses.

Are you ready for this?

And we troop into the kitchen, the kitchen that is dining room and office, bedroom and playroom, maproom and bar. We move the fax and the plastic dinosaurs and squeeze together as best we can, each accepting a tortilla, filling it with refried beans, guacamole and the incendiary salsa, rolling it into an untidy parcel. Daniel has grated the zest from a lime. The two white cups of the fruit lie on the cover of the route book that my daughter has made.

To adventure, we shout.

To the road.

And we lift our Snoopy mugs and toast the night and the grenadine moon.

*

Look, the attorney says. Put yourselves in their position. You wake up in a trailer or some broken down hogan. It's already hot and it's getting hotter. You poke your head out the door and what do you see?

She gestures with her hand.

We look to the horizon but there is nothing there. We turn around and try another horizon. Nothing. We are nowhere.

In the heat of Tuba City she delivers her soundbites; waits whilst Mick obtains his tracking shots, and repeats her descent of the courtroom steps until her walk is right. And then she is gone to another case, another interview, and we are left to an impossible search for a drink.

No map admits it, but thousands of square miles of the south western USA are delineated as the 'Navajo Nation'. This means that even in Arizona, life is measured by New Mexico time. No alcohol is legally sold within the Nation although plenty is drunk. But I am driving now, rushing the Astro down a desert highway, past the galleons and cathedrals, negotiating the native kids who deliberately ride their bikes at oncoming vehicles, laughing in the slipstreams of twenty-wheeled Macks that are hauling America through its own Third World.

★

A rusted Ranchero draws up. Two middle-aged men climb down, one wearing a ballcap advertising Tuba City Warriors. They help a woman from her seat. She must weigh less than eighty pounds. About her wrist shines conquistadorial silver. At her throat is a torque that might have been inlaid by some Zuni master of turquoise. Mother and sons walk down the corridor to reception. I never see them come out.

About 5pm I go back to the ward. Sitting in a corner is a sixty year old Navajo uranium miner. Beside his chair is an oxygen cylinder on a wheeled trolley. Daniel is asking questions which are translated by the miner's daughter, who then repeats her father's answers in English. The doctor observes the interview, nodding every so often as the miner reaches for his mask and draws from the tubes.

After a while our interviewee begins to cry, a tear shining on his chainharrowed face, and because he cries, his daughter cries. What is there to do? he asks.

He had spoken to other white people who had filmed him with their cameras. They thanked him and never came back. All the miner wants is to take care of his stock. But that is impossible now. He breathes through the transparent mask, bony frame racked. On the wall behind him is a series of X rays: his cancer maps. This man had crawled on hands and knees down a tunnel into a mountainside. The tunnel was dark and he had to feel his way. For a period he had done this every day of the week, every week for two years. He had missed the festivals and the feasting of his people, but there was work to be done and such work fed his family. And now he was dying, with no-one to tend the animals.

So the miner breathes his oxygen and the Sony sucks him in. When he and his daughter leave, we give them one hundred dollars.

For the animals, we smile.

They never say a word.

★

We clean up at our motel and take a taxi into town. There is rattle-snake on the menu and jasmine in the air. Santa Fe belongs to us.

Don't know where you're from, says the barman, but my margaritas don't come in pitchers. A pitcher of margarita is gonna be swill. Stands to reason. But I'll forgive you this time. Seeing as.

Mmm, I think. Kaktus Kate wouldn't like that. Back in Cottonwood Kate concocted the stuff by the gallon. I thought of her tavern, the counter so long and the room so dark you couldn't see one end from the other. But we'd found no sanctuary like it from the afternoon glare. Now the barman draws closer, leaning over in his whites.

Wanna know the secret to a good margarita?

We are breathless.

It's the ice. Not that cornmush in a dixie-cup they'd give you in other places, but real rocks, and in a glass so chilled you can hardly hold it.

He draws back, as if expecting dissent.

And the glass is vital too. Not a tumbler but an extra-wide champagne bowl with a salt crust, a real crust, round the rim. Because salt is the real secret. And getting it to stick is all part of the art. You seen those Bohemian glasses out of Czechoslovakia? The ones with a half-inch real goldleaf band round the lip? Salt like that Mexican salt, still with a coarseness to it. Badlands salt if you can get it. Now that's the real secret.

I thought it all depended on the tequila, says Mick.

Got to be the best, comes the reply. None of that industrial El Paso stuff, but the real juice, hauled out of Guadalajara. Clean as aloes on a summer morning. There.

He puts down the tray in front of us. All have ordered different varieties of the same species. We sip from crystal dishes as outside the red street is turning black.

None of your pitchers here, says the barman, an artist who recognises an audience when he finds one.

But you know the real secret of a good margarita? I mean the real secret?

He comes closer.

It's the lime. Always the lime. Gotta be hard and green. Like those little rubber balls they give invalids to squeeze. And wedges, not slices. Always wedges. Welcome to civilisation.

★

"The Alexander Valley Wappo destroyed all their belongings before going to Clear Lake to await the end of the world.

"When the dancing had continued for two years, and the promise had not been fulfilled, the Wappo were disillusioned. Sick and hungry, some of them dragged back to their old haunts in Geyserville. There was nothing to come home to, except to begin again."

In the garden the cheeks of the squash are turning gold. A melon vine creeps twenty feet across the lawn. Cassandra has gone indoors to fetch water, and the others are around the Sony suggesting what might be wrong.

Earlier in the day a camera technician had handed the DSR back to us saying he was afraid to try anything, he'd never seen one like it before. Phone calls to the dealers at home ended in frustration. So we stripped the camera and reassembled it, and I read Yolande S. Beard's *The Wappo: A Report*, a matter-of-fact elegy for the first Californians.

The state's native peoples had been isolated and disorganised. Their resistance, first to Spanish, and then American settlers, had been minimal, and most tribal societies had vanished. Driving west and then north we had come through Paiute and Western Shoshone reservations, but the San Francisco area had been a place of extinctions.

The Wappo's mistake was to inhabit one of the most fertile regions in the world. Because of it they were now forever culturally incommunicado. The bright side was that Napa Ridge Zinfandel might be drunk as a toast to the bounty of their homeland. After discovering the '95 vintage we had pursued it through thickets of Californian reds. Our toast might have been 'To extinction!' After all, it was a bloodied soup of a wine, its grapes nourished in a boneyard.

We decide what is wrong with the camera will last the whole trip. We change the head on the tripod and fit the camcorder. It will be nothing like TV quality, the sound might be poorer, but will have to do. Cassandra settles into a deckchair in the vine-ripening sun. She is twenty-seven years old, putting on a little weight. She doesn't walk so well now.

Some days I can't take a block, she apologises.

The authorities say it is arthritis. She doesn't breathe well either. The doctors say it is asthma. In her lap is a wallet of photographs. At the action sign she begins to talk before a question is asked and we have to call her back. But she continues as before.

They said come up to the Highway. You TV people call it the Highway of Death. They said come up and get your souvenirs. And oh boy, I got mine. But first thing is, you have to understand about us GIs. So first you have to know what GI stands for. Ever thought about that? Stands for 'Government Issue'. They own you and can do what they like with you. So the whole war was an experiment. You know those mannequins with no eyes they get to drive cars? They call them test dummies. That was us. They did the H Bomb on us. They did the syphilis on us. They did the LSD on us. Now they done the DU on us. Listen, that was an atomic war and nobody knows it, and all I'm thinking about is, what happens when I have kids?

An aeroplane is going over and we interrupt the shoot. Cassandra throws down her photographs like a hand of brag. We sit in the grass and pass them round.

The supplication of steel.
Tank-driver.
The Koran.
Young girl.
Barbecue ash.

If the Sony was working we would shoot them as stills. As it is, we squat under a redwood and request the negs. We look at each other and ask who wants to follow the dust. The yellow dust. But the aeroplane has disappeared and we have to start filming again.

The Thief of Baghdad

THE FIRST NIGHT, which will be like every night, I attach the Sony batteries to the battery charger and plug the charger into a socket in my room. The camera carries three batteries and all need to be healthy. Three green lights flicker.

Every morning I deliver the recharged Sony to Nazaar, a cameraman. Sometimes he works for television but such employment is rare. On the first day we talked money and then I opened the bag and revealed the DV cam. Nazaar is a Betamax man and had never seen a digital camera. I switched it on and the numbers tumbled over their screens. Nazaar picked it up like someone else's child.

He filmed the Tigris beneath the balcony. Then the crescent moon on the mosque, the blade of a scimitar. And now Nazaar loves the Sony with its lights and playbacks and effortless zoomography. He is its guardian. Every morning he waits for us in clean shirt and polished shoes, accepts the Sony with solemnity, allowing me to keep the tripod and mike. With Mohammed as our guide – because no-one travels without a government guide – he leads us under the date palms and into the heat, a dapper man, greying, soon to be a father again, a monthly twelve dollars rent to find on his home, and three dollars coming in. Maybe this will be a better month.

Mohammed is based at the Ministry of Information. If we want to go to the British Cemetery or the Museum of Modern Art or the hospitals, Mohammed fixes it. If we seek officials in the ministries, he tracks them down. But sometimes, in taxis, or over coffee, he relaxes. One day he tells of his brother who served in the army during the war with Iran. On one of the fronts the Iranian infantry was so depleted that children were called into the lines. But there were no weapons to give them. Instead, the children were issued with keys that they carried on chains around their necks. With these they advanced on the Iraqi positions. It didn't matter if they were killed. The mullahs told them that the keys were the keys to Heaven. If they died for their country they would find salvation.

So, shrugs Mohammed, they were shot in the battle. Then of course they went straight to Heaven.

And Mohammed sits at the table with his coffee unsipped and tears of laughter streaming down his face.

It proves a two puncture day. After we repair the first our taxi turns off the asphalt down an unmade road. Within a mile we come to a mosque with two blue minarets. A minibus draws up and a party of pilgrims emerges. The mosque stands over a shrine that has existed since the third generation after the Prophet, but our own pilgrimage lies uphill. Ploughing through loose earth we gain the summit and walk two hundred yards to a wide crater. In the sides of the crater a few fragments of brickwork can be seen.

I think of Peter Brueghel's masterpiece, his mediaeval skyscraper collapsing during an earthquake like some Los Angeles multiplex in a disaster movie. That is the only image, apart from the Bible's, that I might have constructed of the Tower of Babel. Until this moment I had considered the Tower a biblical myth. Yet I am assured that these bricks, and this quarry, mark the site. We stand half a mile from Babylon, looking down on the ruins of that civilisation. Fabulous Babylon too is real after all, the dust of its temples cool in the shadows, the mythical animals of its wall paintings facing northwards along the Street of Processions.

And to the north is an edifice that might have given even Brueghel pause for thought. Two miles away the palace of Saddam Hussein rears over Babylon and the surrounding district. It is a fortress from science fiction, a monument in which grace and brutality exist together, and multiply their power by that juxtaposition. Babylon's lions and eagle-beaked dogs confront a monument that diminishes everything else on the Euphrates plain. They pay homage to a colossus. There stands Saddam's Versailles.

Now the traffic is murderous. Nissans crowd the junctions, impatient as robberflies. Trapped amongst them are lorries with raised exhausts, buses painted with the moon and stars, come south from Kurdistan. Yet eventually we reach the sculptor's studio. Vivaldi is playing, the rooms are heady with oxy and thinners.

Mohammed Ghani's work has been exhibited worldwide. He built the Peace Door at the UNESCO centre in Paris. Now a single image obsesses him. He portrays Iraq as a female shape. Its head is microcephalic, the breasts white skittles, the womb cavernous and abandoned. The woman stares down at us from her emptiness. By the twisting of metal the sculptor has fashioned a ghost.

We drive on to the *suq*. Tomahawks might have fallen here but the *suq* itself is indestructible. It is as old as trade. Children follow us through its labyrinth, the Sony on Nazaar's shoulder devouring the mounds of dates, the yellow hauberks of the fruit already browning, crystallising as sugar; past the aubergines, the grapes, the fishmongers showing off the barbels of villainous riverfish, the twenty times used Pepsi bottles in their sinks of meltwater. Lifesavers these, no question. On one day of filming the temperature reaches 110F. I follow the camera dehydrated by diarrhoea, twinned with the *jinn* of thirst. Pepsi and a can of date-sweet Fanta, rummaged from an icebox, keep me vertical.

So *shokra* to the Pepsi Corporation, the most welcome US imperial invader. And the Sony continues through the alleys between the butchers' stalls, their joints black with bluebottles, the butchers' children with their switchsticks defeated by the attrition of the flies; past the ice merchants, the women who unwrap sheaves of coriander and the women who weave plaits of garlic bulbs and cut cuticles of garlic out of their paper skins; past women in head-to-toe black and men in the *jalabiyah* or CK signatures; past handcarts of rice and trays of excoriating peppers; past the man who fills cups from a vat of tomato puree, and the man who unwraps lozenges of soap, as clear and irregular as a honeycomb, hauled in by his Toyota pickup from Damascus the night before.

And then past the smokesellers. Because the *suq* is a democracy of smoke. Normally the most non- of non-smokers, I am seduced by the *najila*. Tea and smoke, smoke and tea, that is how, if there is a little money, time can be tamed in Baghdad. The wick of the brass pipe glows in the dusk. The coals turn red in their nest of silver foil; and the water in its bulb murmurs from elsewhere, like an aquarium filter.

Every time I take the pipe the smoke tastes of vanilla. And the other smokers are always serious. Smoking is a serious business in

Baghdad. I too take it seriously, exploring the trajectories of the smoke itself, my own comprehension of the levitational arts.

And now it is finished, although it will never be finished, this cabaret of fear and welcome and studied indifference our presence induces in the market. There seems no question about it. The *suq* will be with us forever. The Tomahawks may target El Rashid Street and queue, like buses in the sky, waiting to fall upon Palestine Street, but no matter how devastating the explosion or crushing the defeat, the *suq* will re-emerge, one lemon, one date, one smoke-ring from the beribboned *najila*, at a time.

We drive on. At the edge of the city we meet government men with black moustaches and white shirts. Parked in a stockade we stand beside their pickup while admittance is sought to a building. Yet all I can think of is the carpet I had seen in the *suq*, a carpet in scarlet and brown with a pattern of ziggurats on which a figure was visible, climbing towards the sky.

Not any carpet, the merchant had claimed. I had agreed, but shaken my head. The journey home would be difficult enough. It would be impossible to cope with the burden, no matter how tightly the merchant's boy rolled my prize.

But such a carpet. I saw it beneath my feet, or better, on a wall at home, the ziggurats built where the desert flowered around the Euphrates, green as a cricket pitch running all the way to Basra, a river country where the names of stars burst like pomegranates above the boulevards of Babylon.

I walked away from the carpet stall and knew I could never go back. I cursed myself then and today I repeat the curses. But in the stockade where dust blows out of the east and the ground echoes from subterranean machinery, I imagine I stand once again at the carpet stall. For surely that was me, the figure I had glimpsed on the embroidered tower, climbing towards the garden cultivated at its summit, a garden of figs and grapes small as ivyberries, the view encompassing all the known world. Surely I was the figure I saw. But anonymous, minute.

Now a man calls us into the building. At my feet the carpet has disappeared and there is only cement. This is the pumping station for the east of the city. We tour the plant, speaking to workmen who toil at the gears, concocting repairs to them from scrap metal.

There are no spare parts now, and these ingenious men, black with oil and bandana'd like Hollywood bandits, are proud of their work and fearful of the limits of their skill. The pumping noise is so great that they mime their conversations, smiling at us as the camera roams through the thickets of pipes.

Okay, Mohammed says. Downstairs now.

I look at the reaction of the engineers. They still smile but their smiles are serious.

Not us, say the government men, and laugh, but I know I have to go. The chief engineer beckons and I descend behind the cameraman.

There are thirty grilled steps with a metal rail. We climb down into darkness. I know we cannot film but I am forced to look. I understand that. This is the test.

After the thirty steps we stand on the edge of a lake. In this light the lake surface is all I can see. There is no shoreline, only an unbroken blackness like a starless desert night. Nazaar has wrapped a scarf around his mouth but I have nothing to mask the fumes rising out of the crypt.

And I think, we should be climbing to the garden. No man should work in such a cave by such a lake. And up the steps of the ziggurat I climb, the steps worn by five thousand years of pilgrimage, and there is the garden, and a table waiting with a carafe of sherbet, and my mother breaking bread as she did all hours of the day, breaking bread for the bee-eaters and orioles that live in the garden, flinging bread into the air and over the grass for the hoopoes that swoop and coo in the garden at the summit, the morning birds, the evening birds, bread falling over the ground like appleflowers as far as my mother can throw it, the bread flying around her head, and the orioles almost mechanical birds that circle her in the garden from where now I can see rivers stretching from horizon to horizon.

The pumping sounds are louder. Nazaar stands a step ahead, scarved like a Palestinian, leering at me in the dark. There is another staircase that leads further down into a tunnel perfectly dark.

I will if you will, say Nazaar's eyes.

My teeth are pressed so tightly together I cannot say a word. And though I am holding my nose with both hands, the air still forces its way in, the air that is filled with the sulphurous pollen of poisoned sunflowers. Because that is what I see. A field of black sunflowers, all turning their heads towards a television screen where a man smiles and says all shall be well. He is a handsome man in a lounge suit: then a smiling man in a *jalabiyah* taking tea in the desert: then a warrior under the green star: then a tourist in Swiss-style porkpie hat and hunting gear: then a commander surrounded by the snouts of machine guns: then simply an enormous face with a boot-black, slightly fuller than Hitlerian moustache. Leader of his people into destitution, Saddam Hussein has so far appeared in every room I have entered. Every official has a photograph on the wall, a photograph on the desk. But I remember a grave in a modest cemetery. This was Enver Hoxha's grave, a paranoid absolutist who had created the dystopia of Albania. The grave bore nothing but the name of the deceased. Someone had placed a single sunflower there.

We stop way out east. Holding a bucket, he comes towards us through the glare. Beside the road is a field of refuse where goats chew plastic bags. It is 2pm. Dust-devils redistribute the rubbish. The heat is foundry-like. But nothing, says Nazaar, compared to July. Then it was 130F. The hospitals had no air-conditioning. The old people panted like dogs. With no spare parts and no electricity the sewage plant could not pump the effluent. And you know what that means.

Now the boy reaches the stand-pipe and begins to fill the bucket. His name is Ali and he is seven years old. At the Ministry of Information we were told that the average Iraqi child consumes three grams of protein per day. The African average is eleven grams. But that is Iraqi information. Mohammmed laughs, then starts talking. There are more children than cockroaches. The schools are without paper, the hospitals lack medicines, but there are always children. He has five of his own.

If he is unlucky, Ali will die. If he survives he might hawk tapers or cigarettes in traffic. If he is lucky he may sell the big striped watermelons. Or herd goats in the rubbish field. And if he is very lucky, Ali will find work like the man who now passes, riding a cart of gas bottles. He will drive through warrens like this, tapping a spanner on the bottles, the poem of the gas man welcomed into the houses of the poor, his donkey waiting at the roadside, shackled with a stone.

★

Soon an orange-and-white, exhaust gases coming through the floor, is taking us to a suburb. We stop at a building protected by fences. I should know where we are, but changes in the schedule make this an unknown appointment.

We are met by a middle-aged woman. The black she wears is of mourning, not custom. She lives in a caravan beside the building and earns money as a guide for visitors. Nazaar points to a plaque that explains this place was built by a company from Finland. We enter through steel doors massive enough to secure a bank vault. The woman carries a torch and we need it, for the building, whatever it is, is barely illuminated, and empty, it seems, but for rubble. Pillars send shadows into a greater darkness, but on the walls nearest us I begin to decipher bouquets of plastic flowers, soccer shirts.

The guide leads us further in and we stand around a pool of daylight. Above our heads is a jagged hole in the four feet thick concrete roof. Through the reinforcing steel we see palm fronds and behind it, Baghdad's toxic sky. In one corner of the ceiling are curious shapes.

Are they bats? I ask Nazaar.

Instead of answering he tells me to look at the photographs. Then he explains to me where we are.

But I have already been here. By courtesy of television. This is the Amiriya bunker that was targeted by cruise missiles and smart bombs during the first Gulf War. The BBC had broadcast a news conference in which US High Command had shown the Finnish blueprint of Amiriya, its air shafts and other entry points. Military technology was so well developed that a smart bomb had been launched which had entered the building's ventilation system and so, we were informed, destroyed the target. The raid was a success. I remember feeling a mixture of pride and wonder, jewels in the gut, as the bombing technique was explained.

I don't recall asking then what the significance was of Amiriya. Now, as light pours through the smart bomb's entrance, I start to find out. There are photographs here, some of old people, most of teenagers. Amiriya was a bunker where civilians sheltered during the forty-two days of bombing Baghdad experienced in the first war. There are four hundred photographs on the walls, all of them people incinerated when the bomb ignited oxygen canisters stored in the shelter. Our guide lost eight members of her family here. Since then she has dedicated her life to explaining the secret of Amiriya. Other photographs show what was discovered when the fires went out. The heat had welded the doors to the door frames. There were no escape routes. So the children's bodies were fused together as blue clinker.

Nazaar moves round the walls, the Sony on his shoulder, the only light the smart bomb's skylight, our guide's torch, a few electric bulbs.

Up there, he says, pointing to the ceiling.

Not bats. Look.

I strain at shapes or misshapes in the gloom.

Hands. People were tearing at the concrete with their hands. Trying to get out. They died on each others' shoulders. When the bodies were pulled clear, the hands stuck to the ceiling. Black hands. Black hands of the children of the mother of all wars.

Sketches under the Duomo

Years later, Dante was to die in Ravenna, as unjustified and alone as any other man. In a dream, God told him the secret purpose of his life and work; Dante, astonished, learned at last who he was and what he was, and he blessed the bitternesses of his life. Legend has it that when he awoke, he sensed that he had received and lost an infinite thing, something he would never be able to recover, or even to descry from afar, because the machine of the world is exceedingly complex for the simplicity of men.

Jorge Luis Borges. Trans. Andrew Hurley

1

HE OPENS THE DOOR and shows me the room. How large it is. One mirror, one table, one television. And space. Space to walk, to pace the evening boards, space on the table to spread papers or bread and the almond-scented San Gimignano. Number one on the door and the first room I have seen today. The first omen.

I ask him the price, for a night, for a week. He tells me and I calculate and surely he has it wrong. Surely this room is far too cheap for the price he is asking. I look at him and he repeats the figure and I take the room, peeling the notes in my mind, thin as prosciutto.

In the bathroom the toilet is set on a tiled stage. The bathtaps are brass spokes. I hold them as the steam rises and the bells growl in the Duomo. I hold the taps and water rises around me, up to my waist, my chest and then my neck when I lie back. The taps are fully on. I like the water's thunder in the darkness, the darkness lit only by one tea candle on the sink, its reflection caught in the mirror. So there are two candles. I close my eyes and they burn still. As the water thunders. I hear it begin to splash on to the tiles under the bath.

I will think instead of the meal I must make. I will look outside and think of the lizard like a rocket leaf this morning on the Via

Bandini. Its eye was a ball bearing under the skin. How suddenly it deleted itself from the day.

2

Consider the artichoke. Purple, green and bristling with knives. Even when its fangs are drawn it reveals more teeth, like something Sigourney Weaver encountered in *Alien*. Consider the artichoke, the royal onion, therefore best pickled, its mummified white hearts common on the *vinaio* counter. But there are also peppers and tomatoes in this basket: juice-filled, seed-filled wombs. And cucumbers, ridged and gnarled. Because no skin here is smooth or unblemished. No flesh unripe or overripe. No green not becoming orange, no red not becoming purple, no purple not besieged by black, no black not green. Here on the kitchen table with the light streaming in from the Via Bandini is Toscana's bounty. And the blade is ready, the oil, the eyelets of the salt. So taste now. That is the imperative. For God's sake, taste.

Such is my feeding Firenze. For the author, cooking is much like writing. But too often the ingredients taste better than the meal. And maybe teaching is also a culinary art. That's what I felt earlier today at the Villa le Balze. Its students were some of the brightest people I have ever met. But as I sat in the library and watched a blackbird in and out of the wisteria that hangs around Triton's soapstone grotto, I developed a formula:

Repetition = Heaviness
Heaviness = Depression

It's my fiftieth year. Hair greying, wineskins under the eyes. So that's my equation. Now I know what to avoid. This morning I shuddered to think at the times I had given that writing workshop. Yet how the students wrote. Seth from Wisconsin is already a poet, he tells me. On an hour's evidence that is true. But my mind was within the wisteria that hangs over the Via Bandini. Its flowers were the colour of the mini-Vesuvius within a bunsen burner flame. All of Fiesole looked on fire. I was also thinking about the Convent of San Francesco at the village's summit. Enter and on your right is a painting – *The Mystical Wedding of Saint Catherine*, by Cenni di

Francesco. Saint Catherine is about to be transformed. She has grown light as a child, light as a single atom. For surely transformation is the process of attaining lightness. Because as the soul lightens, it lifts. When it is light enough, it flies away.

3

Lying down I can see the Duomo. When I look up it appears so close that I can lift my hand and touch it. Touch the Duomo, soaked in streetlight, the marble of its facade green as the Arno. Once when I awoke it filled the window. Now I sleep with the shutters open and the curtain pulled away so that nothing interrupts the view. And the Duomo comes closer, until it is almost within the room.

Surely the next time I wake the Duomo will lie beside me in this bed. Green and black, its marble. White, its saints. It will lie next to me in this room. The Duomo itself, breathing through its bells, Brunelleschi's dome, feverish as a child's brow, Brunelleschi's dome cupped in my hand.

Down the steps I go out of the Hotel Versailles. And yes, he is here again. The silver man. With the crowds who wait to be allowed in, he is here this morning as he is every morning. A man painted silver.

This man stands so still in his silverness that I might think him a joke, a madman. But there he is. Even his hair is silver. I look at the shape of his skull and all I see are silver curls like key cutter's swarf. Not only is his hair silver but its roots are silver and the skin of his scalp the same. And his eyebrows are silver and his eyelashes are also silver, the strokes of a silver pen.

Sometimes when I pass I look into the skin of his throat and that too is silver but its wrinkling tells me he is sixty years old, the silver man, a man who has seen life and knows what it means, a man who owns experience. And because of that experience this man has decided to paint himself silver and stand like a statue on the steps of the Duomo.

So this morning as I always do I look for a bag or a cup in which to throw my money but there's nothing here. If money exists for the silver man he shows no sign of wanting it. You, silver man, I say to myself, I would give you silver, all the silver a pocket could hold. Is there nothing you need?

Now, around the silver man the Senegalese traders have unrolled their Botticellis. Venus steps out of her shell and into the piazza. There she floats, almost under the feet of the silver man, her hair hanging down. But if the silver man sees he makes no sign. What would Botticelli have made of you, silver man? Botticelli in his disgrace, unjustified and alone, who could not die as he knew he should? Botticelli in his agony. Knowing that only death completes the work.

Yesterday evening I looked on as a group of boys leered into the silver man's face. They wanted to make him smile, to make him shout them away. One boy in the stripes of Inter Milan seemed to spit at the silver man. Or maybe he kissed him, the boy in the stripes. Perhaps he kissed him instead. But nothing happened. As if the silver man could smile. As if he would smile. The silver man stood on the steps of the cathedral and the breath of the crowd on his eyelids and his lips could not make him flinch.

One day, I say to myself, as the bells growl in the Duomo, as I push past in the crowd, one day I will look properly into the silver man's face. I will look as closely at him as I have ever looked at anything in my life. And the silver man will recognise me. He will look as closely at me as I at him. He will know who I am.

Father, I will say. Father.

And a teardrop will fall from his eye. It will make a track on the cheek of the silver man. It will hang upon the silver thorn at the point of his chin. And it will flow like the Arno over the Duomo's step between us.

4

The boy places bread on the table. Then he goes to the barrel and fills a carafe with wine. I look at the wine and the light pours through it. I speak one word to the boy and he turns away and I taste the wine and there is thunder in it, the thunder that strutted around the city's squares this morning, that entered my room and sent the clock backwards and turned the bathtaps on.

Such a storm. And now here I sit as if nothing has happened. The storm's lightning scuttled over the Duomo. I saw a thousand pilot lights flicker over the building. They set the angels' hair on fire, hung from the tails of devils in the roof. And not a second between the thunder and the lightning. The storm was overhead. How monumental was its architecture, how quickly built were the cupolas of its clouds. The storm's glass coffins were full of rags. Hail fell out of the sky, cobbles of it, darkening the steps. People shrank under café awnings as the clocks spun backwards past dawn and into darkness. They looked up at the statues on the Duomo and saw the lights crawling over the saints' robes.

The storm rose out of the piazza like a new cathedral and the people under the awnings bowed their heads. It was as if Brunelleschi had returned, Brunelleschi the master who could produce the impossible, whose engineering used dreams, the architect who would use even God in his mortar, in the flight of his buttresses. It was as if Brunelleschi had returned to the piazza of his boyhood, to the café where he had sat with his plans outstretched on the table, a cup of wine before him.

Under the awnings the people cried out as the hail stung their skin. Surely the storm's cathedral was even greater than Brunelleschi's. The storm was built in seconds not hundreds of years. At last the retribution had arrived. Brunelleschi had mocked God. Here was the response.

But then the thunder passed away. The new cathedral disappeared and all that was left was the taste of hail. The taste of disappointment, which is the taste of hail. And soon the square was as full of sinners as it ever was and now I sit where Brunelleschi sat, the Duomo already built in his mind. Yes, here I sit, looking into a carafe of wine. That writer was correct. There is so much in wine. And so little. Storms and cathedrals, a basket of bread. Now, in my glass, I see the boy approaching with whatever it was I ordered. That word I had spoken, a word I had never spoken before, he is bringing it to me within the smoke of his hands.

Ribollita.

That's what the boy says as he places the bowl in front of me.

Such a word. A word I spoke ten minutes ago without knowing what it meant. Or what it would mean in my life. Now here is that word. The word made soup. For *ribollita* is a broth. It steams before me and within the steam I see leaves and beans and bread. Maybe there are onions. Maybe there is thyme. *Ribollita*, I say to myself. Ribble, rebel, reboil. The world made *ribollita*.

Taking the spoon I am about to taste my word, but suddenly, there he is again. The man in the red coat. Through the window I thought I saw a man I have seen several times. Surely it was him. No-one else in the city wears that shade of red. And such a red. There is no word for it. Maybe it's the red of blood oranges. As tonight I know the sky above this city will be full of blood oranges. Or perhaps the red that Cenni de Francesco used in *The Mystical Wedding*. But no-one else in this city wears that colour and now the man has passed me once again. But surely he waited to be seen. How long had he been standing by the window?

I get up and leave and here I am in the street. It is a narrow street and already dark. But I know the direction in which the red vanished. So I walk and soon come to another alleyway and there is no-one there, but I walk until I come to a narrower alley where it feels correct to turn. Washing above my head is hung window to window. There are scooters parked beside closed doors. And yes, the man in the red coat is one hundred metres further on. The washing lines are lower here and clothes brush my face. A woman sits in a window, so close I might touch her. She looks at me from a room filled with flowers. Around her face there are irises, a face that seems a flower itself, her eyes drowsy as bees. And I am running now, and yes, there is the man in the red coat and soon I'm in a broader thoroughfare, and there are men in sunglasses and girls whose hair is dyed the colours of peaches, and the man in red has come down this street, and that is the man turning left and I too turn left and suddenly we are in the square and there is a queue of people, and the man in red already at the front of this line, disappearing into the Duomo.

The only light in the cathedral is candlelight, its offerings at the shrines, a table of candles in the nave. Yet somehow I know the man is near. He is not in the aisles or under the dome. He is not beside the altars. Yet surely there he is. He has stepped into the painting that hangs on the wall of the Duomo, the wall I might touch in my sleep. In the painting the man lifts his arm and the people in the painting turn their heads. He stands in the painting and around him a crowd has gathered because all of us have been following this man. And here am I, also in the painting. I have joined the throng, gazing up as the man in red directs us into the inferno of his poem.

Gad Bless America

I MUSTN'T WALK FAR. It's bad for my breathing. When I cough I sound like a tambourine. These days I am a grown man with a baby's chest. I dream that my ribs are coral and my lungs the wings of a marble angel toppled into the weeds. So I sit in front of the television. Where a newscaster with smogblue eyeliner and hair like bubblewrap is counting down to Armageddon. When nothing happens I change channels. There is an advertisement for a US Army-approved gasmask on special offer at $79.99. A picture shows a whole family, octopus-faced, watching TV in these appliances. The next advert announces the American Freedom Collection, a 'special American Freedom Statement' of pens, badges and flags at $14.99. Not available in the shops.

Fear fills the media. So does anthrax. Its bacilli, like a map of the New York subway system, are now instantly recognisable. The antidote is Cipro, a respiratory drug, and suddenly the most famous antibiotic in the US. People are hoarding Cipro. They are selling Cipro over the odds, smuggling and blackmarketing Cipro's white tablets. Cipro will save us, is the perceived wisdom. When the anthrax bomb goes off in the football stadium Cipro will let us breathe. Cipro will snuff out the suffocating spore. Take Cipro with lots of water, is the advice. And avoid direct sunlight. Help Cipro do its American duty. Meanwhile, a new American illness has been diagnosed. It is Generalised Anxiety Disorder. They call it GAD. Sufferers of GAD cannot rest. Nightmares invade their sleep. They are assailed by images from video footage of disasters that have not occurred. GAD-sufferers know that life has changed for ever. Their fevers and dreams are evidence that their bodies are straining to adapt to a New World Order. These GAD-sufferers are the first inhabitants of the Age of What Happens Next. They are a fine-tuned elite who understand on our behalf what the Age of Anthrax really means, and what omega next threatens Alphaville. Listen to them. They are evolving with the times.

If walking is bad, alcohol is outlawed. But on the jukebox in the Night Café I hear Muddy Waters squaring up to time and the truth. *One bourbon...one scotch...and one bill.* Out of history The Ventures twang a soundtrack for the urban surf. But it's not all the regurgitated past. Some practitioners still hold out. Tonight at midnight in the 181 Street subway, I listened to a whitehaired bluesman singing for nobody. Beside him his wife begged from strangers. He shushed her and scraped his Dobro. Then he wailed, a real wail, straight out of the belly. His wife gabbled, his chords failed, but he sat singing in his lonesome voice. A whitehaired bluesman on the downtown platform at midnight, his guitar broke, his woman gone mad. And singing out of his guts.

I like the Night Café. It proves not all Americans have gymnasium handshakes and baking-soda smiles. In the Night Café a hat hangs on a wall. It is a dirty hat on a dirty wall, but with it hangs a history. A man once came to the Night Café and ordered a drink. He put his hat on a hook. When he left, he forgot the hat. For days afterwards, customers asked about the hat. It stayed on the wall, gathering dust. Some day he'll come back for it, said the landlord, fixing drinks or repairing the big brass fan suspended from the ceiling. Years passed. The hat stayed on the wall. It became famous. People came to look at the hat that hung on the wall of the Night Café. It was good for trade. More years passed. Then one afternoon, a man stepped into the bar. He ordered a drink. He looked around. Ah, he said. There it is. Last time I was here I left my hat. Thanks for keeping it.

Look, said the landlord. That hat belongs to the Night Café. The man who left that hat is dead. Drink up and go.

This story is told by the bartender.

I look at the hat. The brass fan trundles around. Undoubtedly in this world there is a head the hat fits perfectly. Other versions of the tale say the hat was left by Hemingway and Jack Kerouac and the falsetto man with Little Anthony and the Imperials.

No, no, says the bartender. None of them. Listen.

In this world there are three kinds of men. The kind who leaves the hat. The kind who comes back for the hat. He pauses significantly.

And the third?

That's the artist, says the bartender. That's the joker. That's the poet guy. The kind who makes up a halfassed story about a dirty hat on a dirty wall.

What you havin?

In the bus station there are tiny screens on the arms of our seats. Everyone has a set, like in those old style diners where each table is provided with a jukebox selector. In case I miss something I sit down and feed in a quarter. Bob Hope appears. Bob Hope, 91 or 101, the deceased Bob Hope on a K Mart ad. Bob Hope, millionaire, still chasing the godalmighty buck.

I'm off to K Mart, wheezes Bob Hope, a wizened holothurian. Then he vanishes to a tiny star on the tiny screen.

My quarter has decoined.

On the Peter Pan to the Port Authority a teenage couple are writing a song. She croons and improvises. He writes verses into a notebook. Outside as night falls, the lilypools turn nitric, the freightyards fill with the lumber of shadows. By the end of the journey a good part of the song is complete, the girl whimpering the lead, the boy calling the changes, doowapping behind the love lyric. Getting up, she rustles in leather, skinny as an alleycat, black flowers tied into her black hair. They're going to the Four Seasons Hotel to watch Limp Bizkit duck into a stretch. To smell music and money in Manhattan. Already their poem is Number One. Sir Paul and Madonna unite to present them with the MTV best video award. Out of the alleys towards Manhattan they ride, out of Philadelphia's African dereliction, out of the choking luxuriance of its strange weeds, beyond its Wissahickon schists and grey-shouldered Schuylkill, the Peter Pan churning past the lilypools, the freightyards, past the Grand Ams and a blindsided Buick, black and silver as a night-heron in the rain. Now comes the darkness under the Hudson. We're back on the island of stone. Not far away is Ground Zero. It's been smoking for months. At its core glows an alchemic furnace. Below the basements and subway tunnels are incandescent plasmas of glass and lead and uPVC. Their epicentre will smoulder forever because even when it is cold and reconstructed, this part of Manhattan will remain the heart of a volcano everybody knows can never be extinct. As in true alchemy, a transformation has occurred.

Buses are important in the USA. There is a dignity about buses.

My next bus is a Greyhound which follows Broadway's iron kerb into Harlem. It stops beside a bar called Paris Blue. Jazz nitely, it proclaims. Blues nitely. It's only 11 a.m. but already a gang of grizzled renegades huddles under the cocktail sign. I have a feeling that something might be happening at Paris Blue. Something important. Already I can hear the whisper in the neon tube. Maybe someone like Robert Lockwood Jr., who learned his blues at the feet of Robert Johnson, and at 83 is still gigging, is tuning up. But the culture says I cannot go in. To get into Paris Blue I would have to shrink myself dimesize and roll into a corner of the lounge. So we head up Adam Clayton Powell Boulevard past the braid 'n' beadz shops and pumpkins on the fire-escapes, over into the South Bronx, a Third World Country with the aid cut off, and soon we are in the Connecticut woods. Visit Spooky World, say the signs. Next Junction. Visit Hell House, say the other signs. Next to Spooky World. And then the moon is white as a scallion bulb over Country Club Road.

The park is deserted. Across the road, the farmers' market has packed up. Maybe the population has left for a last day on Cape Ann. Perhaps the hickory woods have claimed them. Or there's the chance they are busying themselves at the out-of-town malls with their special reductions on disposable barbecue sets and new books. One of the books will be a Bill Bryson. It will describe Bill Bryson's travels in America and Europe. Of course. That's where the people are.

This town is Lowell, Massachusetts. It is the birthplace of Jack Kerouac. I sit in the park that is dedicated to Kerouac and read the excerpts of his works reproduced on marble slabs. It is challenging for a writer to find himself published in such fashion. Kerouac's verses, illuminated in the 60F, are badly exposed by such giganticism. A woman walks by with a totebag of persimmons. A child passes on a bicycle. Now I am the park's only inhabitant, but the intimacy of the author's words is missing. Kerouac was a proclaimer, but an intimate proclaimer. What might live on the page has no vitality on a menhir.

Still, this is a pleasant location. Lowell is a town eager to attract artists. There is much to recommend it: individual shops, industrial architecture, dark and labyrinthine taverns selling Boarding

House ale. It cannot have changed dramatically since Kerouac's day. Out of my bag I take a book and settle to a chapter. It is Bill Bryson's *The Lost Continent*.

Bryson is a phenomenon. Warehouses are stuffed with his hardbacks. His paperbacks are scoffed on every underground train and aeroplane in the American-speaking world. On American Studies courses in the UK, he is first purchase on the reading list. In her room at home my daughter devours *The Lost Continent*. She packs *Notes from a Big Country* into her haversack to travel to places Bill Bryson has already visited. Bryson is brilliant, says every blurb. He is superbard of the burbs, our onlie begetter of the bad joke America has become. He is the laureate of New World Lite.

More correctly, Bill Bryson is a reductionist. *The Lost Continent* took middle America and dumbed it down, more deeply down, more subterraneanly deeply down than it had ever been dumbed down before. Or at least until the Bryson clones were set loose, with their Lilliputian blueprints, bry-nylon prose and instinctive antipathy to all things imaginational.

Not that America doesn't ask for it. The US has destroyed its history and environment. It delights in the disneyfication of its own psyche. But the US teems with mysteries. Despite the wagontrains, Hollywood and rock 'n' roll, it remains unexplored. Jack Kerouac attempted the task, but *On the Road* is a muddied stream of consciousness, and subsequent works too full of half-baked zenology. But no matter the failure of *On the Road*. Crucially, it admitted the ritualistic possibilities of the US. It paid homage. It praised. It did not reduce but suggested that here was a world where the imagination might blossom. Ironically, it was Kerouac, the homebird, the substance abuser, the self-styled Breton princeling, who was one of the first pop culture invaders of mainstream art. Kerouac's ilk created the climate in which Bill Bryson flourishes. But any study of *On the Road* and *The Lost Continent* will make clear what has been sacrificed in the democratisation of art since the 1950s.

Bryson might be a better writer than Kerouac. But in comparison his ambition is puny. His America is a circus without lions or acrobats. I come from Des Moines, says Bill Bryson. Well, somebody had to. Cue hilarity. But when the laughter has subsided we are left with an unwitting, or witless, desmoinesification of the mind. The possibilities of Bryson's US are stillborn. He apologises. He ironises with exhausting self-awareness. His eyes and intelligence seem fixed on a notional reader on a 747 out of JFK. Got to compete with the laptop and flight movie. Whereas Kerouac didn't give a damn for his readers. If he had he might have been a better writer. But at least Kerouac has soul, even if that soul has shat its pants, is tormented, damned. Bill Bryson could never contemplate damnation. Damnation has no place in his lost continent. How might damnation exist in New World Lite? There can be no salvation in Brysonville.

Kerouac delivers us to some tawdry places. Yet they are vast with possibility. Bryson's Fartville and Coma are not satisfyingly satirical constructs because they are fogged by the author's air of knowingness. Nothing can ever emerge from them. As to Kerouac, it was unknowingness that fuelled his books. The secrets of America.

Meanwhile, in the chapter I read, Bryson travels to Maine. He finds nothing of interest. So he tells us there is nothing of interest in Maine in prose that contains nothing of interest.

Is this art? It must be. Bryson's popularity means whole Maine forests are pulped to print his paragraphs. Never mind. They held nothing of interest. Even for bryologists.

My tambourine is shaking again. I sit in a Sav-on drugstore while the pharmacist prepares my $55 prescription. What was a night-club throat had become an interesting little cough which brought on bronchitis. Now it's 9 a.m. Lou Reed is singing 'Perfect Day' in the antiseptic aisles, the roller-skaters go past, the GAD aristocracy is granting interviews on the tube. When my name is called I am given a bottle of white tablets. The pharmacist urges lots of water, warns me to stay out of direct sunlight. I look at the label.

Wow.

She's prescribed Cipro. Salvation in a plastic bottle. This stuff is gold dust. I'm safe. And I swallow one before I'm through the door.

But days later my voice remains transparent. If it was a drink my voice would be camomile tea. To me it's the mew of the monarch butterfly on its way to Mexico. It's the heartbeat of the humming-bird around the feeder at Bagel Stop.

Watch out, America, I wheeze, waving goodbye from the air.

Because
the drugs
the drugs
the drugs
don't work.

Paradise Park

GOD. IT WAS COLDER THAN EUROPA. That little world in
its locket of ice. Over near Jamhal's a man was setting up a flower
stall. You didn't often see those at this time of year but he said hello
which was fine. Ignoring him was fine too and gave her a buzz
because what does anyone expect? Then she went past the blue
blockhouse and there she was, Sladie Beaver 9T9, in big letters at
the back. Lady that was no way to behave. Better dead than read.
A few kids were hanging about but the teams were already inside
getting changed. For another grudge match. For another world
cup final on the park at the top of the world.

Strange to see the car burnt out. What was missing was the
paint. There was no colour anymore only the bare metal smoked
and rusted. And the roof so low because the tyres were gone. The
wheels were still there but all that was left around them was wire.
Bunches of it like old wreaths in the crem. And the mousetraps of
the brakes. Where the seats should be were the springs. And where
the dash should be was an empty space. All the rubber melted off
the pedals. And on the floor the melted plastic was like some kid's
abortion left under a sheet. Three large chips. Three minicods.
Three gravies. Five bread rolls because he'll be starving after the
match. Three large cokes. And something else. No it's gone.
There's definitely something else but it's gone. I'll come for them
at five. Yes, it is cold.

With her girl and her boy she goes to the library behind the
security fence and the librarian releases the door electronically.
Thirty minutes later they have the picturebooks in the shopping
bag: a blue giant; an artist's impression of The Singularity. Must be
a hell of an artist. She goes down Merlin and this time almost forgets to look, even though the day is clear. But at the corner she
points. There is the sea, white as a steamiron's hotplate. Then
between the houses her children glimpse the three headed creature
which is sometimes there in the ocean. Then the thin line of silver

like the ink for Christmas cards drawn along the shore. As far as you can see. As her mother said: You've got the views so make the most. On a clear day.

What you wear is who you are. Out of the metal bunker they come and it could be Inter, could be Real, because the kits are that good, yes immaculate, the keepers leaping like harlequins, clapping their gauntlets together in the cold, the captains gesturing already at phantasms that await down the touchline or across midfield, and the referee is in black as if black was neutral – but when was black ever neutral? – and no linesmen, it's not that important, the professionalism here is in the intent, in the ritualism that starts by standing naked in that blockhouse, tightening the strap under your scrotum, already shrunk red and wrinkled as a peachstone, then pulling the shirt over your head, fingering its strange insubstantiability, and the number on it more exciting than your own name, for you are now 1 or 2 or 7 and you possess all the arcana of that number because you carry its spell out into the proving ground, you are branded with your number on Paradise Park, where the earth soon will be more pitted than the thin white daylight moon that rides the bay, by the fusillades of studs, that iron hail, by men chasing their own lives across a whitelimed field and making such a spectacle that other men will come to stare. In their black fleeces. Will come to judge. In their black balaclavas. Men turned loose with time to kill. Thinking that maybe this will be enough.

She pushes her breasts against the counter. Where her daughter with glittery eyelids is dangling her feet. Where her son is playing with the vinegar bulb which she always liked to hold herself. Because of its dimples, cold and prickly. So she picks it up. Too good for vinegar somehow. And there is the salt cellar she can remember the man in school said looked like the constellation of Orion. Like the Ford, remember. If you looked. If you really cared to look. If you stood out on Paradise Park on a winter night and looked over the bay. Weather and everything else permitting. Because he knew there was always a lot of everything else. Or turned the other way where there was less streetlight. To Polaris over the hills that rose blue as mosques from under the mist. And then to the left where the chemical works was brighter than Las Vegas. The fizzing ampullae of an industrial town. Behind them the flame from the steelworks leaning over in the wind. And that man had also said something like da da da the rag and bone shop of the heart. He had read that out. Well, sir, she'd said. That's not bad. But what about the litterbin of the mind? How the others had laughed. How their eyes had loved her then. What she didn't say was that teaching you to think wasn't teaching you to live. Sir. Like how were you supposed to know? Because now look at it all. Are you looking now? Sir?

It's the wind that wins. The wind that terrorises the hill. Low and hard, says 2, but when he launches the ball it blows back over his defence. The striker nips in but blasts wide. How his own side vilifies him, the young man in his armorial silks. No-one else volunteers so he must chase the ball across the mountaintop and into Paradise View. And how diffident he is, away from the white net. How polite with his huge hands open and empty, a little blood already over an eyebrow, the Paradise skidmarks down one leg. There are decorations in every window here, those electric candles beginning to show in the late afternoon. The ball's gone over the reservoir. Some kids get under the barbed wire and bring it back. He can hear 2, guttural behind him. Hard and low this time. Yeah, yeah, wait till tonight. There'll never be an end to it. But it's the wind that wins. It's playing them off the park.

Very dark now. Three weeks left and Christmas decorations in every house. Cartoon reindeer, aerosol snow. Walking away past Our Lady you can see right into the docks. Two ships berthed under the floodlights and the ferry coming back with every deck ablaze. A 13 crawling up the hill. She's got the rest of the groceries from Jamhal's and watches the man on the flower stall pulling polythene off the bunches. He snaps the stems, smashes the heads against the kerb. Big yellow dahlias bursting like belishas. She looks away from a private act. But it reminds her of the time that car went over the quarry. A boy from the special school had taken it. They called him Headshot because he drank vodka and white lightning that his dad bought for him in Victoria Wine. Only fourteen, which was impressive. He rolled the Astra down the slope and the petrol tank exploded. Headshot was good with cars. Screwdriver in the keyhole, crowbar through the steering wheel to snap the lock, then the applied science of hotwiring. Ninety seconds for a Vauxhall, Headshot used to say. A yellow ball of fire gathered itself in the air before bursting into streamers. The pylons behind had been hung with flame. Champagne supernova, like those Chinese poets saw, writing in the light of an exploding star that was brighter than moonlight. Everybody was cheering and then the smoke started coming up thick and black and there were sparks where the bracken had been set on fire and sparks falling out of the sky like tiny hatchlings that lay hissing and blinking on the road as if they might have been alive. She trod on one of the spitting things, a red spider that ran across the slabs. Headshot's greatest moment. Headshot, Headshot, the kids were chanting. King of the Hill.

The books are on the table and the children drawing with the glitter and silver ink. Cards for Nana. Cards for Miss. And in her own book one page open to a black tunnelmouth. In its centre an even blacker point. Where no-one has ever been. Where no-one will ever be. Darker than the rag and bone shop? Oh much darker. Because that black spot was where it was all happening. The Singularity. If she ever owned a club that's what she'd call it. Not the Zone, not The G-Spot, not even the Zodiac. The Singularity. Where it all ended up, time, space, the orange batter round the minicods. Nothing so grand it didn't get sorted out by ultimate gravity.

It's her turn this Saturday so she'll be going. Off the 13 down the Kingsway. Platinum discodiva top from Peacocks above the black splitsided and the black string and the platinum heels. A swab of Heliotrope behind each ear. And the snow blizzarding as the aerosols go to work and she'll never have been so cold as they crowd down Wind Street and into the Passage. She with her Stellas. Kath and Ceri with their Pils. But no chance will they be going anywhere near the football boys because sometimes you think if you hear that *Delilah* sung once more you'll puke your ring up. All over their nice clean chinos. Something singular tonight if you please. So maybe the meteors around the face. Maybe the aldebaran in the navel because it was still there despite the kids. Got to keep the stargazers happy.

The shower's scorching and he goes back to the folded packet of his clothes. So neat you could post it, says Gee, next up the bench. Someone's got an Adidas full of Grolschs and the first one goes down when he's still naked and scalded and if ever there was a cure for what you were sickening for or whatever was working you over from the inside because some bastard thing was always doing that then this is it and put this cold one on your balls says Gee because it's got to be as good as sex anytime and that's what you're supposed to do in saunas anyway you stupid twat don't look at me like that because I never done any uphill gardening in my life ever.

Or maybe it's his turn. So will he be going? In the bathroom he presses himself, hair moussed in twists, sticking up like sweetpapers, a bruise around the cut he got in the game, the proudest thing he'll wear all week. And him barearmed too but not feeling it. The anaesthetic kicking in. He'll stand at the bar with the hundreds, the thousands, the younger ones loud, the fortysomethings still blown from the park but keeping up, quieter, watching the dancefloor traffic, who's in, who's stuck at home, if there's a chance, because what's it all about anyway if you haven't got a chance, the dancefloor exhausts pumping out their dry ice, and there he'll be on the screens, on every screen, close up, famous, laughing. Hiya luv. For five seconds. Number 1.

You go.

No you go.

You go.

It's your turn.

You go.

I doanwannago.

Well I doanwannafuckingo either.

Okay no fucker goes.

Brilliant.

Get some kebabs. Get a video. Walk around by the park and realise that this is high as you'll be. Counting the five pences in your pocket you poured out of the Old El Paso jar. Forget the presents get some Stella. Yeah Stella. And look at the city. That orange fog climbing up the hill. Must be radioactive down there tonight. Kath and Ceri and Gee gone down on the 13, snowspray on the bus windows and the flowerbloke's black panicles stuck to its wheels. Then furthest away the ferry. The ferry in the dark like a burning car falling ever so slowly over the rim of the world. Yeah, insane down there tonight. Mad as the milky way.

The Forty-four Levels: i.m. Caryl Ward

WE WENT DOWN IN THE LIFT and I pushed your chair to the garden that doubles as the smokers' retreat. On all sides the walls of the hospital reared above, so that it felt a secret room, tropical with eucalypts and their blue leaves, alien to that place as were all of us. In the pagoda there we sat with the smokers and the mobile users because phones are forbidden on the wards. But such smoke. The place smelt like a wet bonfire. I think you had two in five minutes and how quickly your skin relaxed, the blood coming back, the light invading the eye. Cigarettes must be extraordinary things. Maybe they should be available on the National Health. Even the thought of a cigarette was doing you good as we came through the corridors, tobacco's sweet eureka taking years off your face.

There must have been a hundred butts on the ground, on the window ledges, piled in pyramids in the ashtrays. Our friend was in, I don't recall the name, the man we had spoken to on the earlier visit. Beanpole of a man, grey as his packet of Lambert's. We didn't say much, but I saw him light five. Five big ideas. Really, all we did was listen to the mobiles going, the conversations that weren't even conversations because, as I found out, by the time you step into that garden there is nothing left to say.

But Lambert tried.

Hot out there, he said, gesturing at the sky.

The eucalypts were smoke-trees now, the air a smudged pane.

Summer, you replied. And I'm missing it.

So we looked up through the asphaltic air. Then somebody's mobile rang with the first eight notes of Beethoven's Fifth.

A few fat drops, that's all it takes, and the conductor cuts it mid bar, *Aida* grinding to a halt, sparks from the violins, a little smoke from the brass. And the crowd hisses as it hissed the tenor in the first act, so that he never appeared again, an announcement made that he was indisposed and would be replaced. To which much laughter, applause. That's the crowd applauding itself, Caryl, because nothing's ever what it seems, and there are protocols here I don't understand. The crowd too has its part, having paid for the privilege. But what I sense is, they don't take prisoners. The Arena is forty-four marble tiers and it's where the public watched executions, the last throes of gladiators, perhaps a few Ancient Brits whitening under the woad.

And that's it. The audience holds its candles and we are twenty thousand in the sultry midnight looking at the blue and silver slaves of an alien Egypt, the set only a little damp but ruled unsafe. Do I hiss with the others? I'm so stiff after three hours on the stone it takes all my time to unconcertina myself. The candles are still flickering in the coliseum. Some of these people will stay here all night but I'm out in a throng heading for the opera cafés.

And the mobiles are going, Caryl, the familiar numbers filling the screens, the texts tapped out. Soon it's gnocchi and nokia and young Europe showing its navel to the night and me stirring my espresso into a golden umbilicus and if I look hard enough into that eyelet maybe I can glimpse the roots of the world. Or at least as far as the pavement.

Because that girl is there again, between two thousand year old stelae. Earlier, I watched the father write her words on the inside of a takeaway pizza box, heartbreakingly neat letters, and she holds it now across her lap and catches the coins. He's put oleander flowers in her hair. Christ, even the beggars here have style. Can't tell where she's from, maybe some Calabrian farm gone to dust and prickly pear or bled white by the 'Ndrangheta, but the pitch is a good one and the Guccis have to mince around and as they do it's the women who look and then nudge their men to stump up, no pockets in their gossamer and no money in their satchels, flat as knives.

In the pagoda I watched you watching Lambert. He dropped the cellophane at his feet, crumpled the old pack and put it on the table. What was smoking him? you were thinking, which is what I was thinking. So what was Lambert doing in his dressing gown on a July afternoon when it was seventy two outside and the sky white and churning? The same as you in your wheelchair.

What ward you on? you asked.

When he replied you nodded and said no more. Because that explained everything. In the pagoda all the mystery was gone. And that's what still terrifies. The ordinariness of it all. Lambert stood there, tall and grey in a tartan dressing gown, and offered us both a cigarette.

Coward that I am, I shook my head, but you took the second ciggie from the pack which was silver now and not grey, and he lit it with a stone-coloured flame and we waited in the pagoda and said no more. But I learned about smoking that day. What the language of smoke really means.

Already the waiters are out with champagne for the big tickets. If I had more sass I'd simply lift one from a tray, but I'm a level forty-four man with calves still cold from that varicose limestone where Julius Sixpack used to sit, not bothered about a few drops of rain but calling for the wine-carrier to bring the pitcher down the aisle, for the indisputability of blood.

Thinking of your writing, I understand why Pittsburg never appeared in the poems. The city was all prose – those cloverleafs I can't imagine you driving, the brownstone caverns of downtown. The poetry tells of rootedness – the patch from Bryn Cwtyn to Pant Ruthin – and the people held tight by those roots, by the dawn over Cae Ffrynt and the light in the Ewenni Fach. That patch: a stile in a lane where a child sat to work things out, stitchwort and red campion necking in the hedge.

Bryn Cwtyn is the plover's rise. Now when I see lapwings, that little horn on their heads, I think of your square mile and a bird dragging its wing, drawing the danger away from a nest scraped in the ground. But Bryn Cwtyn is another dream. Nothing was obliterated more thoroughly. Today even the opencast mine has gone, the crater that swallowed the farm itself vanished.

They're building a Call Centre there now. Last time I passed the foundations were cut into mud, a flight of concrete steps ascending to nowhere. A thousand jobs, the hoarding says. Where our children will stare into gold screens and thread voices on a loom. All those connections made.

British Telecom once employed scientists to search for evidence of some form of consciousness in the system. Like something starting to wake. Coming alive. Then they disbanded the team, saying it would be impossible to identify such a state. But imagine it. Every telephone a neurone. Our conversations the creature's bloodstream. Or its thoughts.

A mile down the road from the new centre I came to the church. On the far side I sat on the stile made from gravestones, the one with the word 'here' cut singularly in its face. There were words at my feet too, tombstone fragments in the graveyard path. And sitting in the yews' prehistoric shade, I could have sworn there was some-body close. I could hear them. But after a while I decided it was the motorway. It was the motorway breathing. So I kept still and lis-tened to its exhalation in the gouged water meadows a mile away.

And kept still. As dusk fell the Victorian tombs grew immense. Spired and corbeled, they lay like derelict mansions under the trees. That's a peculiar place, Caryl, where money calls its last hurrah and orange lichen thrives on the wall. The church porch was boarded up. No-one arrived and no-one departed. I felt as if I had listened there on that stile in the darkness for one hundred years.

But we can drown in a tablespoon. There's inertia in that world. No-one where Bryn Cwtyn stood ever pretended much. Pretence and swagger and difference were not familiar, and therefore unwise. But you were working on it, finding the strength. Around here it takes time. Around here, being newborn at fifty is not so strange.

Fine, no Pittsburg. Instead, you told of the white roof of Sony, a frozen lake from the motorway, and ghosts calling ghost cattle to the milk parlour through bloodbrick McDonald's. Pant Ruthin is a Travel Lodge now. Do not disturb. But that was the base, and you were adding to it, building the work.

Sitting in your room I touched your hand. I had never felt skin so cold. Ice to the elbow. Clammy as those Marigold gloves housewives used to wear. Or looked into eyes so white. But I've seen trout in the Ewenni with the levels sinking, one of those sum-mers when the pools vanished, the whole population drowning in daylight. Or that year when the phenol seeped in, colourless as the rain. Sitting in your room I watched you burn down to nothing. Only the bones in your face were articulate. The blue schirrus lay like a cobblestone under your skin.

Soon after, I looked at your work. The cancer poems are hilarious.

I laughed at the cold cap, the women picking out wigs. All over that room your hair had lain in single strands that the sun caught and threatened to ignite, your hair as bright as fusewire around my feet.

I sit with my espresso and the audience streams from the Arena, its floodlit and teetering galleria, *Aida* axed, and the magnums upside down in the pails. And everywhere I look in these illuminations, the sills, the steps, the balconies, there is that same cherry-coloured Valpolicella marble, the walls, the paving slabs, the church porches, the forty-four levels of the world. Yes everything beyond your closed and bloody lids. But you would have followed the child, Caryl, scrunched up now like a paper ball, and seen that even her flowers are the colour of marble and heavy in her hair.

Being Mr Ogmore

But Mr Ogmore was a proper gentleman
Under Milk Wood

Prologue

Luckily, I'm a cheap date. It takes a single glass and I'm talking to myself. So here in this Restaurant mit Tradition I'll say it all, whilst watching the lemon burning in my beer. As good as anywhere to confess these dreams and exhibit the painting of the inside of my head. Because tonight's the night. I'll walk on at Humboldt's Grossbritannien-Zentrum and be Mr Ogmore once again. I will put my pyjamas in the drawer marked pyjamas for an audience of students, professors and washed up yet genial British communists who for solidarity with their German comrades bought apartments in East Berlin and are now forever marooned. Meanwhile, I'm scribbling too. The bargirl, who wears a ballbearing in her tongue, offers a scrap of paper. Because everywhere I go I jot my Dipsomaniac's Haiku. Here's *Last Orders*

Should I
        or shouldn't I?
Perhaps that's why they call it
        mulled wine.

Mr Ogmore at The Chelsea

I was asleep in room 809, my part's pages drifted round the armchair. Dreaming of home. Of my river. Because sometimes at night I stand on Rocan Ddu in the rivermouth and look south. Sirius burns above Tusker Rock. That's my own belle isle, Tusker, a black line in the night, sprockled with foam and starlight. And that's where the Tuskeroras live, the last original inhabitants of this coast, without plastic or iron, strangers to fire, unacquainted with the wheel. They're hardly a tribe now, less than a clan. More like ghosts I'd say, or ideas of people. Yes, ideas of what we were, what we can never be again. That's the Tuskeroras. Speaking their molluscs' language. Some locals claim they're the spectres of sailors lured by wreckers to the reef. But to me they are the last of the first. The rest of us are asylum seekers.

I woke and looked round. Through the window the Empire State was changing colour against an El Greco sky. It's a lost world, this hotel. I talk to the water-bug. My loyal companion. Think of a cockroach on steroids wearing a medieval cuirass. In the dark it clicks like a cooling carburettor. Then it opens its wings and becomes an iron butterfly. That's the water-bug. Outside this room is a labyrinth with a variety of minotaurs, most of them artists, grizzled *djinns* in dressing gowns, sweat pants, NYFD ballcaps, velvet fezzes, Turkish slippers, motorbike boots, Blue Oyster Cult tour jackets, their rent hanging on the walls in goulash-like gouaches, in autopsies in steel and glass, every floor and stairwell boasting its livery of delusion. They'll talk Behan to you, or Hemingway, or marvellous Marlais, sometimes Sid Vicious killing Nancy Spungeon down the corridor, over and over that debauched act, British punk's Dickensian gift to the Apple. How I despised that couple, their imaginations more emaciated than the Tuskeroras on their mussel bed. Vacant souls. But I listen to the legends of the lost. Every year for fifty years I've sat in this armchair scanning my lines, the Empire State leaning across the bed like a doctor with a hypodermic. Fifty years ago they carried Dylan Marlais Thomas through that door and he never showed up again. Killed by a cocktail of morphine and cortisone. So beware the physician with his miraculous bag. He made an orphan of Mr Ogmore.

Mr Ogmore in Ogmore-by-Sea

Who better than me? I have rehearsed all my life for this, matriculating in every Ogmore degree. So who could be more Ogmoreish than Mr Ogmore is? I've fed on oysters at Bwlch Ffynnon Orensh. Considered callisthenics beside Bwlch Caehalen.

Eavesdropped on oratorios in Bwlch Bach. Read the sea's grammalogue at Bwlch Gwyn. Coveted a kite above Bwlch Kate Anthony. Wrought a wreckers' bonfire over Bwlch y Ballring. Given boule a go at Bwlch y Gro. Notched my name in the Triassic wadi's rock. Listened at dusk to a curlew calling curfew as the sea rushed in with its news. And nothing's more Ogmore than that.

Mr Ogmore under the Palms

Here's what I've learned. Wait long enough and the loose ends get looser. But occasionally there is synchronicity. Forty years ago I recall Mr Rees in our boys' grammar school using what seemed a spectacularly inappropriate word to describe a mathematical formula. *Beautiful* he called it. What a Welsh-speaking wally old Sid Rees was. Us tyros of trig thought him a tosser. We knew what beautiful meant. But mathematics concerns exactitudes of time and place. One day I walked out of the desert into Babylon through the gate of Ishtar-Sakipat-Tebisha, built by Nebuchadnezzar II. Ishtar's columns were an otherworldly blue. That gate sent out the Babylonian armies, welcomed in astronomers, mathematicians and artists who would celebrate the works of the creator-god, Marduk, lord of eternal life. Then along Procession Street I went, beneath its bestiary. There was Mr Ogmore, perspiring under the palms, with hardly a part to play. But that Ishtar was largely a replica. A century ago German archaeologists unearthed the original and had it erected in Berlin. Such imperious dreaming. But dislocations like that are common these days. This morning I searched for the Wall and found nothing, only Romanians selling breezebricks they might have grafittied themselves. Then today, of all days, thinking about the performance tonight, I turned a corner in the Pergamon museum and there was Ishtar. I was back again. How peculiar. I felt I'd come home. Is that synchronicity, Mr Rees? Maybe now I understand. Down the reassembled Procession Street I walked under the claws of Mushhushshu the dragon, as I had done in Saddam's Babylon. And I read what Nebuchadnezzar, the wise, the humble, the caretaker had written about the gate's construction. From Ishtar I made my way across Berlin to another portal and stood with the tourists imagining and failing to imagine a darker Babylonian horde passing through the Brandenburg Gate, and a future that would always be the present, but impermeable behind steel, exalted by ignorance.

Mr Ogmore on 4th Street

At Swift's the beermats proclaim "better belly burst than good liquor be lost". So I'm doing my best. While observing the drunks, the desperate, the disingenuous drip-feeders whom alcohol has not yet harmed tonight. Take this toper. Middle management, white, thirty, sub-Ivy League aspiring blue sky thinker. And thoroughly Calvinized. So let's call him Calvin Klean. His idea was simple: one, probably two, potentially three apres office icicles of vodka. But already he's skiing over the Skyy horizon. I enjoy watching him. He makes me want to write, here and now, on the beermat, another haiku. Here's *Guinness*

> When you call for the porter
> expect to get
> carried away.

Yes, I can read his mind, feel it losing its grip on tomorrow when he will wonder why his suit smells of gingko fruit and the plastic's maxxed out. But forget the morning payback. Think Novocaine and able. Because tonight he's a giant in Lilliput – instead of a refugee from Citibank's termite palace on his way up Jacob's Creek without a paddle. Imagine that sigh when he disconnected from twelve hours broadband and was free to head down here to East Village funkydom. Now the saloon at 7.12 pm is like a Rembrandt etching: simultaneous ghostly shading and hi-def particularity. Yes, by some miracle of light and shadow, Swift's front bar resembles Rembrandt's 'Christ Healing the Sick' and surely the executive mind is as sharp as the artist's burin. So keep those stress salvers coming, Calvin: and what about *Vladivar Red Label*

> Three weeks in the freezer
> and every molecule
> still on fire.

Or, dipso facto, *Glenmor to Glendhu*

> He counted thirty malts behind the bar.
> Surely an optical illusion.

I'm reading your thoughts, Calvin. If it wasn't such a full time job being Mr Ogmore I might have played your part a hundred times.

Mr Ogmore on M Street

I follow the fire until water is set down and I feel its grip in my throat. Then it is gone but more arrives. More of Enriqueta's water poured from her pitcher cobbled with ice, the *jarra* that is always full no matter how much of Enriqueta's water I drink, the thirst a companion for so long, as if it was a child grown up beside me to a wheedling man, a stranger who has led me through this city, the cars angry, the crickets in the lots stitching the notes of a harsh serenade until at last the stranger delivered me here to Enriqueta's place and sat down opposite, raw in his red shirt. And now we look together down M Street, the stranger and I, as another glass is put before me, and then another glass that I wish only to smell, because the perfume of Enriqueta's water is more than enough for now, and hours pass and surely days of my life, maybe years, and there is the stranger back on M Street and he is whispering to the sun, that same green fire snaking round the buckles on his boots, the same green flames upon his head like a crown of cilantro, Enriqueta's lover now I know, as I know he is the sun's *mandadero*, as I know although I'll never know how I know that this water is my life story told by Enriqueta, and I must sip from every syllable with my splinter of a tongue.

Mr Ogmore on the Beach

Goodbye, what were you? You were the hare. So, I salute the hare. The hare was with me a long time. Off the dunes I followed the axles of the frost, the sand churned by horses' hooves, down Ffynnon Pwll past Pwll Swil and the pools piebald with ice, then over Pwll y Briton Tom to where oystercatchers were moving over the moraines and sea-rocket ran red this autumn like lava on the beach.

Throughout town the light was unstable, water beneath the promenade a jostle of permanganates and silvers, waves climbing on one another's backs. And for all the next mile only a single creature with me. The badlands hare, my little Mercury of the rock pools, the hare whose home was Pwll Dafan to Gwter y Cŵn, the hare that licked salt from the Samtampa reef and samphire from the fringes of the peninsula's bayous, the hare drowned on the beach, its fur lilac, its eyes inundated, its back legs broken truncheons, a hare alone on the sand and meeting me there for the last time, a hare bereft, his brindled nape and pollen-coloured nap that was a nimbus upon him at twilight gone to iron, the hare drowned dead at my feet, a denizen of Sker thrown back by the sea into a country where no tree has ever grown, hardly arrow-grass and glasswort. A region of caves and limestone clerestories where a hare should properly be a dream.

Mr Ogmore on Museum Mile

West Farm, with the best views in Wales, came up for sale. One August day I stood there and east, west, the sea was seamless, glazed like one of Nebuchadnezzar's turquoise tiles. Out of my league of course. So I squatted on the Rocan learning my lines. Yes, home's a problem. Where is it? On Fifth Avenue I dreamed I would have made a member of the Arapaho Crazy Society. Those sad Arapahos, in death's arabesques around the wagon trains. But a tolerant people. They allowed their comedians to unionise. Arapaho crazies meant the contrary of what they said, did the opposite of what they were told. My perfect civilisation. And the nightmare? Being born on the Gilbert Islands. Everyone was a warrior. When they weren't killing outsiders the Gilbertians fought themselves. No-one was allowed a shield but people wore coconut fibre armour. Give me Tusker every time.

Yet maybe this is home. After the performance I went to Ground Zero and looked through the railings. Nothing but a crucifix-shaped girder on a plinth. I'm surprised there is no effigy of a fireman nailed upon it. The last time I stood there the epicentre was a lobe of mercury pulsing under the rubble. Simooms eddied around South Ferry. This is where America's tallest building will stand, the world's biggest target. But there is colour too, and I collect colours, the purple of my armchair in the Chelsea's crumbling suite, a green habanero sauce from Enriqueta's. At the Met I found El Greco had already discovered those shades. His saints looked down on us, bodies stretched to the ceiling as if racked by the Inquisition, thunderclouds with their bright embrasures massing over Toledo. An apocalyptic imagination, suited to this city. But I stood for an hour before *Boy lighting a candle, with an ape and a fool.* Which am I? I kept asking.

Mr Ogmore in Sainsbury's

Whittling a switch. That's been my life. I spent fifty years in the backwoods, my hideyhole a mattockhead of country bordered by two rivers and an ocean. I tried to make sense of it but sense was never enough. Not far from here the Ogmore river runs in spate, whilst over its moorgrass slides the Odeon's ultraviolet beam. *Lord of the Rings* is coming. *Attack of the Clones* has gone. Next door, Sainsbury's is the old isolation hospital. Before the films I wander its aisles to listen to children's deliriums, to my own childish voice fretted with fear, the faces of the hallucinating and the dying bright under deli glass. On the fever ward they taught me to walk and as soon as possible I tottered away across the moor and now the moor's the motorway. Take care. There's never a silence in traffic's confession. But note a KFC nugget bucket in Coed y Gains. The bluebell reefs in those woods are spectral as Ishtar's subterranean blue and hugged by a blue Euphratean dusk. While above hangs a Phantom with its cluster bombs, like a bridesmaid with two bouquets. For uranium too will know an annunciation. In the atom's stable the infant Christ lies smiling, the Magi looking down their microscopes. Fifty years of sharpening pencils and here I am in the supermarket, asking for cashback.

Mr Ogmore endures Global Warming

I ordered a St Louis at Johnny Rocket's, a retro diner with personal jukeboxes. So I stuck on Otis Day and the Knights, then The

Champs doing 'Tequila'. It was about four in the afternoon when the meal finished. All the clubs in Jazz Alley were closed so I mooched about in the 75F. November heatwave, the air peppery as pokeweed, a riffing of thunderheads over Manassas the news channel warned. Then there she was.

Have you got the CDs? her companion asked the man behind, who raised a plastic bag.

Yes there she was.The last time I'd seen that face was in the Uffizi. It was smiling from a canvas by Botticelli. Now here was that bootylicious madonna, proud as a goshawk, belly taut as a Florentine sonnet. Here indeed was the gold of Guadalajara that The Champs extolled. And she floated along the M Street sidewalk, heading back to her suite in the Four Seasons and holding hands with Tom Jones.

Mr Ogmore at the Reichstag

I was rehearsing my lines in the queue for Norman Foster's dome, watching the figures above enmeshed in a vitreous web. When I looked down there was a crow on the step behind. It was a hooded crow, common in Berlin. I had walked along Unter den Linden from the Palas der Republik. What a monument: built in three years in the 1970s, abandoned, dumbfounding. See it now before it vanishes. The Palas was a bronze railway compartment carrying the dead souls of a thousand sneaks toward their pensions. Exposed around it is a subterranean honeycomb of soundproofed rooms. Now it's a home for crows, the only totalitarians left. Meet them here too at the Reichstag, shitting upon democracy's glass oriels. The one bird beside me is a frosted coal, pale as Erich Meilke in his dress uniform. Meilke, minister for state security for thirty years until 1989, was mastermind behind the *Staatssicherheitsdienst* – the Stassi – that staphylococcus in his bisected country's bloodstream. Meilke and his ilk used paranoia as a weapon. Good day, Herr Nebelkrahe, this cold morning. Remember those winters when the ground was iron and full of microphones? Those Mays when Mitte's magnolias took photographs? Look at the city you have inherited. Such work is being done. From The Fernsehturm, an enormous television tower, the capital's a smouldering atlas. While at Humboldt where I perform tonight the striking students chant. Berlin is bankrupt. Education will no longer be free. University lecturers must take a huge pay cut. So capitalism too must eat crow while the polezei wait in their green and whites. But at least Meilke's office is open to the public. Walk in. Listen to the silence there, its archive tape recordings of snow falling upon snow. Then take a tram to the Zentrum. Tonight I need an audience.

CCTV Elegy for Rebecca Storrs

YOU KNOW WHY SHE WORE a jewel in her tongue, don't you? There are places you should and places you should not go. I've always understood that. But there are also places you have to go. And sometimes one of the places you should not go is a place you have to go.

A slate spun off the pub rooftop and shattered in the street. I opened the door on an empty bar and ordered a drink, taking it to a corner table so I had a view of the room. There was a television on a metal arm hung from the ceiling. A karaoke backing track was playing. I knew the song, 'I Will Survive', by Gloria Gaynor. But the words were missing. I kept waiting for Gloria to start a verse but nothing happened. It felt like a hole in my head. I couldn't remember the words, but my body needed the words to start. Whatever they were.

Nant Ffornwg. Nant Ffyrnig. The fierce stream they called it and I've followed it all my life, down to where it collides with the river, and I mean collide, where its waters break and lose themselves flowing east into those greater waters coming south towards the sea. That confluence is hidden by bramble and shade. No one would guess that there in the darkness is a meeting of strangers, one strong, one lithe, but the turbulence is there for all of us to find and maybe understand. And yes, I've followed it all my life. The fierce stream. Down as far as the place where the waters meet.

I was trying to remember the last time I saw her. It might have been in the corridor coming from B Block, when she pressed the envelope into my hand and pushed past with the crowd of seniors in the opposite direction. Or it might have been that time at the staff room door when I was leaving and she was looking for some-one else.

But something tells me it was when I went through the Drama studio on the way to Art. She was up on stage, rehearsing the birth scene in that play her group was doing, something by George

Bernard Shaw. She lay on her back, crying and groaning and then exploded into laughter when she saw my group trail in. We had to get out because she couldn't continue until there was no audience. She wasn't ready for an audience, she begged. They were only trying out the scene. So I went out but I could hear her behind me. Laughing, then crying. Flat on her back in a black school pullover and black jeans. Trying to get it right, the director telling her what type of pain to imagine, because even pain could be measured in degrees, like the strength of the wind or the purity of gold.

The river crawls from under a stone. It is tiny as a grain of rice. It creeps out of the ground and suddenly it is as thick as my arm and the coldest thing in the world and it runs down a gutter it has worn, hastening now, as if there was anything that could call it back to its subterranean origins, and very soon it is headlong, harrowing downhill.

Darker now. Gary Glitter's 'Rock & Roll Part 2' playing. There are people in, young mostly, and an older man sitting at my table with an *Echo*.

Terrible, he says.

I look at him and he taps the front page of the newspaper on the red formica before us. I can see the face on it, the only face. Straight hair, tense smile.

He leans closer.

You know why she wore that jewel in her tongue don't you? You know why all of them do it these days?

I say I know because I don't want him to tell me. But I don't know.

Surely no-one could have understood those waters better than me. There is a bank where archangel grows and the river seems motionless, dark, with the bottom invisible. It might be three metres deep. I have walked there and stood there, the archangel bowed in its hood, my trail black in the dew.

That was where anglers cast and threw lunchwrappings into the water and watched them carried downstream. Men who worked with fish, their pouting lips, the eyes rolling in daylight. This was where I had once tickled a trout in the shallows, a shiny creature with rusty mottling on its belly, as long as my penknife with the longest blade extended. It lay between the stones and I looked away and then back and it was gone. All in half a second. I was going set it free. But I wanted to hold it for a moment. The silver of it. The freckling. Hold it down between the stones.

There she stood on Friday night, before her bedroom mirror. Fixing the fish-hooks in her face. Screwing the jewel into her tongue, the serpent into her navel. There she stood combing her hair behind her back, taking a shot of Red Flag. Only to relax, to get where everybody else was going to be. But to get there first. Its colourlessness filled the bottle's cap. How harshly cheap vodka burned in the throat. A kind of oiliness. And icy grey if you held it to the light. Something writhing in it. You'd have to be really strange to drink it for pleasure. The oil uncoiling in your mouth. But it did the job.

When her parents had asked for her poem I searched everywhere. There in the stack on my desk I found many things I had forgotten or thought lost. But the poem was not amongst them. Then I searched through the plastic bags of poems that children in that school had written for me. There were hundreds of pieces of paper and hundreds of poems. I had chosen a selection and word processed them and an anthology had been published.

In front of the mirror she tightened the jewel, combed her hair. Then she went into town. She met friends in the Three Horseshoes and Zeana's Kebab House, CCTV following her through Wyndham Street into Adare Street, her hair fanned out in the camera's stony light. That silhouette unmistakeable. Those gestures. When they told you who it was, you could see at once. As if you had always known. Rebecca Storrs. We know who you are. You're unmistakeable.

Who was it found her? A man walking his dog. That's what they always say. A man walking his dog. As if that's the only reason a man has to be in a place like that. But how often have I stood there and watched the river flex its dark muscle, the dyes coming downstream from Fort Saint James, the volatiles and the aromatics out of L'Oreal, the snowmelt, the frostmelt all adding to the flow, the rainwater out of the saturated hills, the adult fish pushing against the water's wall and their smolt uncertain in the alder shade. Or stood and seen the levels were low and the cobbles exposed like tumours in the riverbed where before was only the current that hurried everything away.

★

So why do I come here? To a place I shouldn't come. Because this is where the whispering is. Everywhere else is silent. But here words divide and subdivide like cells under a microscope. They mutate into shapes no-one would have predicted. The whispers run along the walls and through the lights of the fruit machines and out of every bottle suspended behind the bar, and those behind them pushed to the backs of the shelves, their crusted jewels years untouched. Peppermint schnapps. The sedimentary Bols. A glamorous world if we would only raise our heads. And the whispers run into my ears and my mouth and when they reappear I am a different man. I will have heard the whispering and it will have changed me. Its cells in my cells. Its culture dividing in my blood.

One evening after school we read from the anthology, staff and parents drinking wine, the children smart and alert. A good evening, I had thought, but the poem, her poem, was not there. All I can remember is the white envelope which I imagine held the poem, and hundreds of children jostling after the bell had gone. They pressed into the corridors, the sportsbags on their shoulders making them look like crustaceans. Crabbing forward. Crabbing back. But what I did with what was in the envelope is a mystery. There were so many poems, hundreds of them. Every hand offered a poem. But not her poem. So now there is no poem to read at the service. The poem she had taken so long to write. Maybe the last poem she ever wrote.

This is where she sat as the bottles crowded the table before her. Where the man sits now with his newspaper, reading about what she liked to do, the amphetamines she tried to buy.

Oi, geezer, she's supposed to have said.

Got any stuff?

It's in the paper so it must be true. As the whispering I hear now is true, in the machines, behind the toilet doors, the whispering that tells the truth and which I've come to hear. To be close to her, the envelope in my pocket. Ripped as if in rage. The empty envelope I don't remember opening. With my name on it in her black slash of ink.

Because there was no poem a friend read Christina Rossetti's 'Remember' at the service. *Remember me when I am gone away.* That was a brave girl who read that poem. What a choker that one is. And

Christ, the Glitter Band is back on again, one riff over and over, the drama of it, the dirtiness of that riff, the mindlessness of that riff filling my mind. I take a long pull but the music's like a claw in the soul. Gary Glitter with his pompadour peeled off on the dressing table, downloading off the net, downloading the dead. That's what I think about when I hear that music, music I don't want to hear, but I'm here to listen, I'm here to learn. Remember me when I am gone away, the girl read, and her voice is another whisper in the walls of this place. Gone far away into the silent land.

But how often have I stood in the silence with only the archangel beside me. Crouched with the nettles, new and green, that are armed with delirium. I have stood there in the evening and the heron has come down to the bank and lifted its wings like a Cretan windmill and sighed out of the bone of its throat and I have seen far into its eye and what it contained before that heron knew of me. I have stood there in the darkness and the eels have crawled out of the mud and knotted themselves about one another in lariats. They have come out of the water with gills like nettleflowers, the teeth in their jaws no bigger than watchwheels, and they have set off on their journeys into the dewpits of the surrounding fields and when they returned I was still there to witness their greeting of the water as they went to reclaim their territories. River-eels. Mauve and thick as microphones, those expeditionaries, and migratory from this place before the river had a name.

Pils. With that green condom over the bottleneck. Red Bull hurtling through the blood. Such cans and bottles left behind as she makes a telephone call and takes off up Quarrella Road with another group of friends. Party on. And again, the cameras have her, but for the last time now. A stop for kebabs in their polyfoam tray, the shreds of iceberg shaken out. Everyone in that queue she knows. A small town at 2am, you're going to know almost everyone. And they know you. So she goes up the Wild Mill. Where the cameras cannot follow. The Wild Mill by the river that whispers for anyone to listen. Ah, but that is river language. There are few translators now.

See, says the man with the *Echo*.

Iss messages. Iss all to do with messages. Cos iss one here, and he taps the front page, iss one liked giving out.

★

By half three the smoke makes its own space at the top of the room, a blue room where you could sleep and dream with eyes wide open. But lie down and it all goes weird. So get some air. Go out to the riverbank.

Now there's a different Gloria song playing. Gloria Estevan and the Miami Sound Machine. But the words are missing and the hole is gaping in my head where Gloria should be singing about bad boys. How she loves those bad boys. But there's nothing and it throws me and I'm second-guessing Gloria and she's winning every time and anyway it's the Sound Machine brass that is getting the punters moving at the bar, the bad boys laughing down at us from the nightclubs, their tropical estancias on the screen above our heads.

A man looks up. The whispering has stopped. Even the river is holding its breath.

Oi geezer.

Yes he has for her what he has for her. A handful of salt. A crystal ball. Name what you want, name anything, and someone will have it, someone will be waiting with what you think you need. Because this is the magician with a coat full of corridors.

Much has come past on the current. An armchair once, riding the spate, and I imagined sitting there enthroned as king of the river, all the way through town with people cheering and lining the riverbank and throwing roses on the water. As they threw roses not long ago and watched them carried towards the sea or catch on stones, one by one the petals coming off. Nothing broken so quickly as a flower upon that shouldering swell.

Good sounds at the party, kid. Things you never hear outside the clubs. They kind of remix your head, DJ Goldfinger, DJ Mr Ed, laying it down. But we all need a breather. So let's go to the river where it's quieter than here. Let's go there.

The man opposite offers me the paper but I don't need to read. I can hear the whispering instead, all around the room in the blue wires and the brown wires and the green root stapled to the wall and plunging into the ground behind the jukebox. 'Rock & Roll Part 2' is playing again with its sound of jackboots marching to a door, its gruff commands as if a crowd was demanding something from itself. Then willing the something that appears, that it squeezes out, to show itself.

Thass what he said, says the man at my table. Across the red formica. The paper've put it in a special box. Read what that man told his butties.

But I've read it before. I've read everything that man is supposed to have said.

I gutted her like a fish.

That's what he said. It's in the paper. In a box. Words that reach out to you with their nails and teeth. Body piercing words. The scars they leave. The streptococcus that goes round and round in the blood and you imagine there's no harm done. But there is. There always is. A culture carried everywhere the blood can flow. And then it poisons you.

Oi geezer. Remember me when I am gone away. Gone far away into the silent land.

Outside, there's a camera slowly panning the street. But the street is empty. I think of the stone-coloured street on the screen of the CCTV. And not a soul about on a night like this as another slate comes off in the wind. No-one in Zeana's kebab queue, no-one waiting in a doorway with a view of the comings, the goings. Not a soul.

Crying or laughing. Who could tell? Not me as I hurried out of the Drama room. Maybe I was holding the poem and maybe I wasn't. But perhaps it was a letter, a letter for me, because who could tell now what was in the envelope? And then there was another hand that waved a paper, and another, and this was a nest of poets, unquestionably, just as there was one behind me louder than the rest who was laughing as she gave birth, shrill as a magpie on that stage, the splinters in the black wool of her pullover and her hands between her legs as she pushed for the baby to come and pushed for the baby to come, delivering that ghost of herself into the mercies of this world.

Scherezade

THE FIRST NIGHT I LAY DOWN on my bed and listened to the city. Soon the traffic had dwindled to a few taxis so that I could hear the river, a highway itself with the city lights upon it, the river flowing through my head, its rats, its roosting egrets, its bargemen who had always travelled at the river's pace and made their lives accordingly. Getting up, I could see much of the city, including several mosques. Nearby rose a mosque that seemed larger than the others, with a floodlit dome. I turned off the light and stepped out on to the balcony to watch the minarets glow against the sky and bats flit about them, crazed messengers out of the polluted darkness that seemed to pass straight through that golden hemisphere.

On the chair were the towels she had brought, the maid in her black uniform, a woman with black hair and black eyes, her cheekbones rouged and on her lips a smile, curious at first, but then wide and white, an unapologetic smile that was almost a laugh, a laugh for this stranger who handed out money as if that was his aim in life, to give all his money away.

The second night she came without towels. There was a knock on the door and she stood there smiling. She was rouged and tall with her hands at her sides like a schoolgirl in her uniform. Come in, I gestured, and she came in and looked around and straightened a cover on the chair. And stood there laughing. She was laughing now, the first person in that city I had seen who laughed. If it was money she wanted it was money she received. I counted four of the black 250 dinar notes and she accepted them with grace and laughed and left the room.

The third night she knocked again. It was an urgent knock and I hurried to the door. She spoke and I shook my head, unable to understand, although her smile was the smile of the previous nights, so wide and so white. She gestured and laughed and I asked her to come in. When we stood in the middle of the room she took my arms and stepped to her right.

Yes, I said.

Yes, she said.

Then holding my arms she stepped to her left.

Yes, I said.

Yes, she said.

Then she held one hand to her ear. And laughed. And still she was the first person in that city I had known to laugh.

Yes, she had said, and let me go, her hands at her sides against her black dress, and out of my pocket I offered four banknotes and she took them and they vanished immediately and she turned and left the room.

In the city that day there had been a wedding. Now there was a wedding feast in this hotel and at the end of my corridor the brides and bridegrooms were dancing. There was a conference room there and the one hundred and fifty couples and their guests were dancing through the evening, quietly at first but gradually more fiercely, as if daring the night to end, the tablas so loud and fast that surely those goatskin drummers must soon exhaust themselves, the shakers of each ringing *deff* throw up their hands and call for the tapes to start.

Unable to sleep I walked up the corridor and stood at the dancers' door. The brides were silver and blue, each one wrapped like a chrysalis in her silks. Their grooms wore the orange and red of monarch butterflies. Such finery, I thought. Such richness here at the end of my corridor, so close to the room where I was trying to sleep. So I looked through the door and the guests called me in. But I stayed outside, the music quickening now, the dancers twisting with the ringing of cymbals, the dulcimer's powerful incense in the air. And always the drummers, the drummers carrying the dancers along and the dancers looking to the drummers, the drummers to the dance, as if to see who would be the first to fall exhausted from that race.

The next night she knocked and I opened the door and she gestured to come with her. We walked down the corridor and two flights of stairs, the carpets crimson under our feet. Soon we came to a room and she opened the door and drew me in. It was a small room, lit by candles and veiled lanterns. I turned back for her, but she was gone and a man approaching. He took me to a sofa and gestured sit. Another man brought tea in a small glass, red tea with a little glacier of sugar within, tea made with limes, from Basra the man said, the way the Basrans make tea, for he was a Basran too, and tea with limes was a delicacy only he might prepare in this place, the steeping of that tea in limes and limejuice.

When I had drunk, another man approached. He led me to the side of the room where one red lantern burned. There were cushions here and many pipes, some old and carved, some large with pale waterbulbs. He gestured to choose a pipe and I pointed to a tall *najila*. That man kept a clutch of coals in a piece of aluminium foil. Selecting a coal he blew on it and lit the pipe and brought the pipe to my sofa. And there I sat throughout the night, listening to the water in the pipe, sucking smoke and breathing out, taking the smoke deeper with each breath until I felt it reach my lungs. But already it had found my head and I knew that I could move like smoke, a smoke-snake along the ground and under the drapes of that camp, because the room was decked like a Bedouin tent. Or I might fly like some smoke-falcon above that desert place and look down on myself with unblinking eyes.

The fifth night she knocked and I opened the door and she was holding a book. She smiled and I invited her in and she sat down in the chair where I usually sat and placed the book on the table between us. She pointed to pictures of palaces lost and discovered and maybe lost again in the desert, to photographs of men who had dug into the sands and come upon temples and granaries, scholars of this city with teams of sunburned labourers. There were pictures of tombs and ziggurats in the river territories and she then turned a page and pointed to the Street of Processions.

Yes, I said, and she said yes, but I said, no, you must understand. I stood there today in the morning light and the griffins looked down, those fantastic creatures looked down as I walked along the Street of Processions, my own slow procession through Babylon, blessed and cursed by those creatures that have seen so many passers by, the griffins, the eagleheaded dogs. I pointed to the pictures of that bestiary. She smiled and said yes, but I said no, you don't understand, I have seen them, these creatures, high on the walls looking out, guarding the approaches to Babylon, stranger than any man could dream. But she closed the book and stood smiling and I took one thousand of the black dinars and made them her reward.

The sixth night she knocked and I invited her in. She was holding a postcard and put it in my hands. It was cracked and brown, a postcard that a visitor might have sent from this city years ago, before the wars. I had water ready and two glasses, water in a sealed bottle, but she smiled and did not drink. Tonight she seemed impatient and pointed again to this new thing she had brought.

It was a picture of the Lion of Babylon, monumental, ringed by visitors. How this woman can read my mind, I thought. Yesterday I had walked through the deserted city. Dust blew across palace floors, stone crumbled in the desert wind. And not a soul in Babylon but Nazaar the cameraman and I, dragging our shadows in a black frieze across temple walls, the strata of Babylon buried beneath our feet, deeper than the Euphrates that heaved itself through the floodplain to the north.

Perhaps it was the wind that blew, the neurasthenic desert wind, that made me feel like a moody child, but I was hauled by a whim of my own foolishness around that place. Then, in the north of the ruins, I turned a corner. Immediately it was there, the black lion, abandoned it seemed by Babylonians tired of its celebrity. Or returned to where it belonged, out in the desert air and scouring wind. Now nothing announced the statue but its own ferocity. Here was the Lion of Babylon escaped from the museum world and as raw as when the artists cut the last strand in its mane in that basalt block four thousand years ago. The Lion of Babylon free once more.

The seventh night she led me to the mosque where the bats flew. We removed our shoes on the steps and a guide took us through a room where men knelt in prayer. Above our heads the dome was a dark planetarium. Then we entered a whitewashed room. Against the wall was a shrine to the Prophet. Around the shrine were heiroglyphs like the flight patterns of bats that spilled on to the floor in a cryptic alphabet. There was an old muezzin there, who gestured at the black-stained walls.

One day, he said, a group of men arrived at this mosque. They killed the priest and they killed the boy who served the priest. The marks you can see around this shrine are writing made in the blood of that boy. I say it is writing. Yet there is no proof because no-one can understand it. But I think it is writing in the language of the murderers. Mountain language, strange, with primitive letters, writing that was only staunched when the last drop of the boy's blood was shed. Our interpreters have tried to translate, but they cannot. And until we understand what they have written, we will not wash it from these walls.

The eighth night I was late back. As soon as I had shut the door and set the camera to recharge I heard her knock. Before I knew it we were past the hotel gatekeeper and a taxi taking us away. It pulled up at a building where a man opened enormous doors and beckoned us in.

Welcome, he said. You are the first visitors here for many months.

Surely I've been here before, I replied, but she took my hand, the first time she had ventured this, her own hand small and cool in its black sleeve, and led me room to room.

In the first chamber an artist sat painting. Before him were arrayed rows of tiny figures made of clay. He dipped his brush in a pot of crimson oil and touched the first figure. Then the next. But such a task, there must have been thousand and thousands of such figures, uniformly grey and naked. They were mounted on shelves and in cardboard boxes stacked to the ceiling. The artist showed no sign he had seen us. I stepped softly to where he sat. Before him where a selection of brushes, some of a single hair's breadth. But the pot, I saw now, was not filled with oil. The artist dipped again. On his brush was the gleam of blood.

In the next chamber a woman was polishing the floor. She crouched on her knees holding a rag.

If no-one comes here, I asked, why does she polish so hard?
Nobody replied.

At the end of the room was a Cruise missile. It was mounted on a metal stand and reached above my head. There were US markings on its white barrel, the nosecone painted in black and white checks. Standing on tiptoe, I could stroke the tip like the muzzle of a horse. Then she spoke.

This was a missile that flew down Palestine Street, I saw it myself. It passed down the avenue like a firework at a feast, a long white missile. It seemed to be lost, it flew so slowly and so low as if it was searching for something, peering into the windows of houses as it passed. You could see the writing on its sides. It landed behind the houses near the market. I waited for the explosion but there was none. And now I look after the missile and see it comes to no harm.

In the next chamber, wall hangings of red and gold were suspended from the ceiling. There were rolls of carpet against the walls, and rugs and embroidered bedspreads upon the floor. A hooded man stood before us, a hooded falcon on his wrist. As we passed, the bird attempted to rear up. Its wings spread out in a dark baladaquin so wide it seemed to fill the room. We hurried on.

The next chamber might have been a schoolroom. There were smashed desks and chairs whilst the floor was covered with broken glass. At the far end a woman wrote with chalk on a blackboard.

What is this place? I whispered. Where are we?

The woman turned. Why ask what you already know? she replied. This is the Museum of the Mother of all Wars. You are most welcome.

The next night when she knocked I was ready. I had washed carefully and put on clean clothes, but if the city's dust was in my shoes or my hair I trusted she would allow that I was a man who spent his days working in the heat. Gently I invited her in and she came smiling, her arms at her sides. I motioned her to sit and she frowned at first but I said yes and she said yes and then she sat down and smiled. I looked at her cheekbones, rouged again, perfect crescents like the crescent moons I saw in this city, high up on the mosques. I was about to speak but out of her breast pocket she took a photograph and handed it to me. It showed a baby naked in a cot.

Everything I knew she understood. Or so it seemed. That day I had walked into the city hospital. The pharmacy was empty, not a bottle on the shelves, not a bandage. On the first ward four men lay awake and silent. The air conditioning had been switched off to conserve power and at their bedsides wives or children fanned the air. Out in the street there were glittering pools where effluent had come up through the drains, electricity being cut to the sewage works. The men looked at me without regard and I passed on.

In the next ward children lay on plastic mattresses, no sheets or bedding, their skin in that heat grafted to the sweating plastic skin. The doctor I was with asked Nazaar to film a sleeping child. This infant had been born with a rare cancer and would not live. Nazaar brought up the lens and rolled the film. There was a tap on my shoulder. While we had been filming the sick child, a sick child behind us had died. Its parents had hidden it with a towel. The family stood weeping around the bedside but when we turned the camera upon them they stood to glassy attention. One yellow arm, one yellow leg showed under the cloth. Nazaar ran the camera over the bed. The mound was so small I would have sworn no child could have lain there.

I held the photograph and smiled at her. Then she took it back and left the room, the black banknotes already concealed.

The next night I had made special plans. When she knocked I invited her to enter. On the table I had placed a dish of melon and pomegranate. There was bread and a Pepsi with a new screw top. I urged her to eat but she shook her head and hurried me from the room. This time we went down in the lift and out through a back door. It was dark but still warm under the palms and we walked quickly across a road commanded at each end by the statues of heroes, then turned into a car park. I tried to speak but she gestured to be quiet and we entered a maze of streets more intricate than the *suq*.

After a while the houses were gone and we came to a gate in a high fence. Even in darkness I knew where we were. Beside the gate was a machine gun emplacement protected by sandbags. Three soldiers sat smoking. That afternoon I had stood before the gate and asked admittance. The corporal had smiled and shaken his head and then walked off to reprimand his troops who were playing football with local children. Now my companion whispered to the corporal. One of the soldiers opened the gate and she led me in.

We walked down an avenue of palms. On either side were aisles of gravestones that led away into the darkness. We stepped through the grass that streetlight had bleached until we stood in the middle of the graves. Every aisle was the same, and every stone. I knelt in the grass to read and saw one name. John. I walked to the next and knelt again. John. The third grave was the same and after ten I gave up. Every aisle was the same and every stone and every name the same.

This was the British Cemetery. The soldiers had died in a distant war and their graves not been seen by relatives for many years. But everything was orderly, the grass cut, the weeds pulled and left to shrivel in the sun. It was hard to see in that darkened place and perhaps I had read the gravestones wrongly. So I felt the lettering with my fingers and thought I touched invisible words, words that might explain. But maybe the words only existed in my head or were from another language. Yet I wrote them within my secret book. Then she touched my arm once more and led me to the gate.

The next night I paced my room waiting for her knock. I wore my last clean clothes, and had counted what remained of the money and replaced it in my shirt. Outside the traffic streamed over the bridge and the moon rose behind the dome of the mosque. On my table were a dish of figs, a dish of dates and a bottle of *arak* with which we would toast each other. I could imagine her smile as she tasted her drink, hear her laugh as we finished the elixir.

I combed my hair and combed again and at last I heard her at the door. Throwing it open to the corridor, I brought her in, laughing, for I had tasted the *arak* to make sure it was suitable, and there she stood and I was astonished and stepped back. Tonight instead of her uniform she wore a dress long as a *jalabiyah*. The robe was midnight blue and on her breasts were sewn stars and flaming suns, and the rouge on her cheekbones sparkled and her eyelids were painted midnight blue and there were rings and bracelets on her hands hung with galaxies.

Look, I said, and showed her the *arak*, the dates, and took her hand and led her to the couch. Here the camera stood on its tripod. Beside it were the cartridges of films and my film-maker's numerology scrawled on a hundred sheets and my secret book filled with its forbidden words.

Here is everything I've seen, I said. Everything is recorded faithfully in these hours of film. The city, the desert, the busy ministries. Everything is here. Even the terrible things you cannot possibly have known. See them as you drink. So look here. And I motioned her to the viewfinder where everything that had been filmed could be replayed on the tiny screen.

But she laughed and taking me by the shoulders stared into my eyes. I could feel her breath upon my mouth, smell the bergamot on her skin. She came closer, her breasts with their stars against my chest, and her rouge painted dark. I held her waist and looked into her and saw the desert in her eyes. It was the desert I had crossed to enter this city. I looked away and looked again and there was the desert of Badiet Esh Sham, black and petrified.

In that place nothing had grown since the making of the world. The earth was a black glass and everywhere stones lay upon it as if meteors had fallen and cooled and now lay as black scoria to the horizon. And I was rushing through that desert, travelling west away from her, past a truck stop where traders lay on beds beside the petrol pump, past a shepherds' cairn that might have stood a thousand years.

I looked into her eyes but I was falling farther away, and I spoke to her, held her close, but the words I was speaking were the words of border protocols, and her body that I held so fiercely, the waist so slender under her robe, was the camera I had packed in a bag of dirty clothes and no larger than a cradled child.

Outlook and premonition

The Outlook from the Kingdom of Evil

All day the doctrine of the dove
Is crooned from a cage behind the house.
What can it mean, such bittersweet
Language, that there is joyfulness in gaol,
Or that every generation grieves
No matter how distant the defeat?

When darkness comes, the roost's at rest,
All laughing thoroughfares are still;
But through the marram sways a psalm -
The dove is welcoming the dawn,
As captive in the hand of God
It dies for us beyond the dune.

Wil Ifan: *In Porthcawl.* Trans. Robert Minhinnick

THE PSYCHOS? The mythical murderers? They're friends of
mine. Here I am again at the entrance to their museum. Inside I
can hear their voices. The fairground's crowded but there are few
takers this summer's day for the hamfisted horrors of the
Kingdom of Evil. For this type of evil anyway, the cartoon evil of
dripping fangs, psychotic eyes: a demon with a manky hound.
Meanwhile in the laughing thoroughfares, the Welsh working class
shows off its tattoos, its NY ballcaps, the Nike tick of approval on
every shivering tit. But there's good trade elsewhere today after
months of rain, the trippers back and fore between the Megablitz
and the caravans that stretch into the dunes.

Those are the dunes that intrigued Wil Ifan (1882-1968), a
lyric poet if ever there was one. He discovered that from their
cooling finials you could follow the constellations all the way down
the southern sky to the black rim of England. Or triangulate
between Venus and Cog-y-Brain, one of the highest dunes, and the

lighthouse. Such a place. Where the lover and the lapwing as well as the astronomer might sense immensities growing about them out of the sand. Where the Milky Way drifts off like conger fishermen's campfire smoke. A place before the Kingdom of Evil offered its vicarious thrill. And today a place where the neolithic survives under the neon, and the bronze age is palpable.

Back in the fair, the newspapers wrapping the chiptrays describe another evil. Iraq. Because Iraq is part of the USA-identified 'world axis of evil', war against evil Saddam is inevitable we are told, Saddam whom I'm surprised is not here today, a waxwork in the wax Kingdom, a canister of nerve gas in one hand, a nuclear attaché case in the other. Saddam, with his mascara'd moustache and devastating smile. Smiling Saddam, potentate and all-purpose panjandrum of evil, here with the poisoners and the perverts. And the paedophiles of course, that other royalty the Kingdom now boasts. And still, in the unaccustomed sun, there are few takers for the train through the colonnades where murder waits and blood's a bucket of ceramic gloss.

Outside the fair is a wire fence with a *No Trespassing* sign. As no-one's looking, under I go. This used to be the dinosaur park. Now the tyrannosaur has gone but its jurassic garden remains. Porthcawl's microclimate of burning breeze and saline drip-fed sea-fret allows a little exotica to flourish. A multitude of palms was planted here to provide an authentic habitat for lifesize plastic raptors. Those palms have now matured into a tropical copse known only to mitching-off schoolkids and Special Brew-for-breakfast topers. If the dunes belong to another time, this woodland's from another world. Wil Ifan might have thought himself transported to Jerusalem. But I'm reminded of somewhere else.

On El Rashid Street I counted the palms: the bent, the benighted, the suffocating palms of Baghdad. It is pollution that's killing those trees, the leaking exhausts of Baghdad's traffic. I counted the green palm, the yellow palm, the black palm. Then I counted the pyramids of dates beneath. And then the children with faces as colourless as datestones. Their generation is growing up with a fomenting grudge, a whole generation malnourished in everything but ideas of survival and ultimate revenge. What was it the Minister for Information told me before the lights in her ministry packed up and an imperial guard of cockroaches invaded the toilets? There used to be three hundred species of palm tree in Baghdad. Now there is a third of that figure. While many Iraqi children exist on a quarter of the necessary calories. We are propagating terrorism in the mulch of children's bones.

Later, from my attic, I watch a machine called the BeachParty spin couples around the sky. Corkscrewing like a firework, it endlessly enthrals. And because it is August, a voice exhorts the townspeople to visit the Kingdom of Evil. Even as it speaks it warns us of the fate that awaits us there. But tonight I'd rather watch the airborne lovers. There they fly, over the caravans to the edge of the dunes. To the Arabic alphabet of the stars. Close by, under the palms, there are plinths where the dinosaurs stood. Only their footprints remain now, big as birdbaths, but I remember the creatures' eyes, red as the dates on El Rashid Street.

The fair is ramshackle. But it's sleazily compulsive, a dangerous place, full of sex and terror. How we love to be terrified. And what's sleaze but a dirty mirror? Look into it if you dare. My daughter used to work in the fairground as a cocklegirl. She sold trays of seafood to the laughing families, the loitering loners. Which terrified me, most nights. For all its absurdity, I say long life to the Kingdom. So maybe I'll go there tomorrow. Maybe I'll see Saddam.

Burning Season

THROUGHOUT EUROPE the heatwave continues. In Pen-y-fai, Wales, I pick a peach from my mother's tree. It is sweet and wormy and I enjoy it as much as a peach from Malaga market or the glorious brimstone-buttocked peaches of Pecs. Meanwhile, in Seville, people die on the street. The temperature reaches 124F. In Portugal, wildfire runs through the cork oak.

What should we do with this? I ask my mother, of the plastic urn that contains my father's ashes. It has stood on a chest of drawers in the hallway for seven years, hidden behind tins of catfood.

Maybe I have heatstroke. I think I'm delirious. Which is good, because that's how I prefer myself. I'd like to scatter my father in the ferns on the mountain above Deri, the village where he was born, in a colliery-manager's house, large and removed from the throng. He used to hide in the fern forest, that pudgy little boy, a third son in three, thus disappointing his mother. Who told him so. I don't think he described anything as vividly to me or with such longing as that Rhymney fernhill, green and oceanic in its currents: not the thunderclap in Burma when slogging down the Mawchi road he heard about Hiroshima, nor the eye of the English hurricane he found himself within in 1987, when fifteen million trees were blown down around him as if a meteorite had struck.

But in Porthcawl the sky darkens. Thunder arrives like punishment, angry, male, halting our sundance, sending us back to techtools and screensavers. Lightning is a white crow's foot over the funfair. At my office door on the high street, the locals are scattering. And who are these young women, I wonder, tattooed like Scythians, racing their buggies out of the rain? Fifteen years ago on a day like this they would have been camped with my daughter on our back lawn, playing 'Papa Don't Preach', eating Curlywurlys.

Cloudburst or not, the fire edges closer. The newly designated nature reserve I walk most evenings is reduced to charcoal. And what's this? This whispering, this whoomping under my feet. As if twilight was not enough or high tide not enough, nor the swifts enough as they scoot like potassium about a sky almost as dark as themselves, the swans arrive and in their hearts is the sea, their racing reflections stored by the sea for future use, locked away knowledge and a memory of swanflight, evidence of swans for a time when there will be no swans but swans in stone and silicon, and swan DNA guarded behind steel doors. But for now here are swans in a sky that already contains the red sun, the cuttlefish moon, two swans whose necks are stretched sunwards, neck-stretching swans six inches above the waves, the cuttle-whitened waves, the cuttle a huge harvest tonight and these swans' voices the night's canticle, these sea-swans stretching from one world into another, and from the unbeknown they race into my dimension with their whooshering and their whoompering, two swans against the grain of the waves like two white teeth gripping a bone, two white teeth of a bandsaw against the tide's growthrings, and there they fly – two swans into the blackness, the waves pillow-pounding the karst and releasing these diamonds, the cuttle in and out of the moonlight and the swanwings wheezing like harmoniums, whooshing, whoomping, these swans beneath me under the cliff, their sky beginning a millimetre above the waves, the swans' course northwest to where the sunset vanished, for they are launched, these swans, their eyes skua-swift skewering the darkness, while in their hearts is the sea as the sea is in their racing reflections.

The next day is hotter. Thunder has scattered itself over the waves. But observe the gleam. And under heat's stupor find a frenzy. This is a feverishness I value, like my father's Burmese diseases, which remained with him all his life. They put him in touch with something out of bounds. A weird dream licence. At least that was malaria, with all its malarkey.

But when was the last time I felt so transported? It must have been a year ago. I entered a room in a terrace in Vilnius. There were poets there. Hours later these visiting writers had gone but the Writers Union had come alive. Here's all I remember. There are women dancing. Their eyes and mouths are malarial. There are men dancing, spinning, drunken, bearded and bearlike. There are politicians, there are prostitutes speaking Russian. There are artists of all species and all of us are caught up in the dance. And such anarchic jiving and jitterbugging, such chilled-out, loved-up, stoned swaying it is, before becoming headlong and headbanging once again.

Lithuania recovered its identity. And is in the process of renewing it. Meanwhile, the Pen-y-fai peach tree's leaves are darkening, its fruit red and sclerotic. I remember planting that tree, a peach-stone sucked by my sister of its last shreds, dibbed in and forgotten. Blissfully, in that garden, I seemed to grow up with no sense of national identity whatever. Nobody talked of countries. Ideas were more interesting. Maybe that's the first step to freedom. Or the ultimate stage of oppression.

The fires run on across Europe and no border stops them. Milan experiences its highest temperature and the Zillertal glaciers retreat. Delirium deepens. Newspapers in the Ukraine reveal a man has carried his twin, alive, inside him, for over twenty years. I think about that incarcerated child. Another man's body its bony senate, a brother's whispering blood its liturgy. As I'm a twin, the notion is bizarre. Yet it's not a National Enquirer sensation but a medical fact. And maybe, I think, that's nationality now: that's nationhood: a primitive prisoner within all of us, an unbearable foetus writhing beneath the heart. Maybe that's what it means to be Lithuanian in the twenty-first century.

On a shelf above our dance sat a poet. Or rather this poet reclined, left hand cupping his chin. He resembled a diabolic cherub. How eagerly he studied us. I knew the poet was American but could not remember his name. Perhaps I should have seen him as Falstaff: an outrageous, sybaritic presence. Or rather, a lord of the dance. No dancer himself, in shorts and tartan shirt, he swung from his perch a druidic crozier. There had been thunder in Vilnius after a hot week. Rain flooded the culverts around Katedros aikste. Soon the dance had to end, our dream dancing, but while he could the poet spurred us on, shouting appreciation, waving his glass of *bajoru*, a man who had discovered a powerful place, a centre of magic, of release, both joyful and angry, after genocidal times.

When my father was dying my mother sat singing by his bed. She crooned all the names of the cats they had kept together. She pummelled his chest, pleading with him to wake, but he was a man beyond us all by then, unreachable by the farm cats they had fed, the stray cats adopted, the nervy Siamese for whom they had constructed silken pavilions. His malaria almost over, a soldier was dying who had never known a country. Or: that soldier's country was found within his mind; a country I'm only now able to recognise. The country of an idea.

The reserve, like the Portuguese cork forest, is ash under my feet. Meanwhile, swans ride on the high pressure swell between Gwter Hopsog and Ffynnon Wen, their throats red-black as the wombs of Slovakian chilies that hang on my kitchen wall. Soon the cuttle harvesters will be here with their sacks, building the cuttle stooks over the beach, but for me the two swans are still flying, still reaching for the next dimension. Then maybe the one after that. And they're passing straight through me to get there.

The Outlook from La Tuque

TRY THIS. STAND ON A CORNER in Winnipeg. Count the people. Soon you'll discover no matter how many people you count, it doesn't feel enough. So move west. But even in Vancouver's markets it's not enough. Go east, to Montreal's rush-hour. Still not enough. Still no critical mass. Because Canada has an emptiness at its heart. Canada's an unfillable country. And you know that over the horizon the emptiness begins. No bad thing maybe. But in La Tuque the emptiness gets eerie. It's like the cold. No matter the sugar ecstasies of autumn, the symphonies of La Fugue, you know the cold is coming. It was 25C yesterday, the Saint Lawrence arterially blue. Weird weather, but the weather is always weird now. I shut my eyes and sat in the Saint Lawrence sun. But I was thinking about the cold.

It's all because Canada is supersized. Like its food. You don't get fries in La Tuque. You get a bucket of fries. You don't get a burger in La Tuque. You get a doubledecker with bacon and Monterey Jack. And pieces of iceberg. See what I mean about the cold in Canada? Then satchels of mayo. Suitcases of ketchup. Order a pizza in La Tuque and the shield of Achilles arrives. With a 64 oz. soda. Yeah, supersized. A bit like Jeff. My new friend.

I'd been heading north for hours. It was time I stopped. I had an idea there might be nothing else, ever, in that direction. So I stopped in La Tuque and met Jeff. Jeff is a translator. He works on the Net at home in La Tuque. He loves the Net, its urban drawl, its tribal catechisms. Jeff is the future. He's also bilingual. English, French, he's in and out the two bushes like a chickadee. Total immersion, he says. So now both languages are instinctive. He can think in both. But usually he thinks in colours. Or in masques that are finished in nanoseconds, even with encores. That's how we really think, he tells me over our wine. Not in words. So never trust a translator, says Jeff with his supersized smile. Translators will sandpaper your Christmas. They'll demonise your patio. You can translate but you cannot translate. An oak and a maple both have leaves. But they don't taste the same.

Jeff and I are in La Tuque's town hall. This passes for café, theatre, gym. Tonight there's jazz and La Tuque radio is coming live from the concert.

Awesome band, says Jeff.

Language too in La Tuque is supersized. But the music's good. The drummer has a personality that dances on the bass pedal, skates on the snares.

Then at 8pm the La Tuque news is broadcast live in front of us. It's going to be cold, says the news. It's going to be dark. It's going to be empty.

I look at Jeff.

D'you ever feel isolated here?

Not now, he says. Not with the Net.

Jeff is big. Jeff's an ensemble all his own. Jeff's a drive-in mega-family-meal combo deluxe with extra icecream. And plenty of iceberg.

Isn't La Tuque a long way from anywhere?

He smiles again. Not from the Net it isn't.

Jeff's not worried. So I say to myself, if Jeff can live here, maybe I can too. Property's dirt cheap. And property means a pension. I could afford a second home in La Tuque. Maybe the locals wouldn't mind. Of course I'm not bilingual. I've never been totally immersed. But I'd have my own radio station. It would be my retreat. Every writer needs a retreat. In Canada they pay writers to retreat. One day it will be compulsory for all Canadian writers to retreat.

What d'you translate? I ask Jeff.

Porn, he says. Hockey history. Irritable Bowel Syndrome.

The jazz has finished. I start thinking again. About the cold. Because the cold is coming. From the north. The terrifying north. Where the emptiness is. Where the ice stands in line at the drugmart grinding its teeth like a wolverine. Where the darkness waits in Fuddruckers' parkade. In that old coat. In those old boots. Where emptiness cruises all the way up Main Street in a black-glassed humvee. Then all the way back down.

Casino tickets, says Jeff. Positron Emission Tomography.

Awesome, I say. You're the future, Jeff.

And Jeff orders us two more glasses of Niagara Peninsula red.

Native Perennial

WHAT A MARVEL IS CHALK. I walk on chalk and talk of chalk. You're all chalk, I say to the dune that rises above me, to its hollow crown, its viewing platform of sand. And the chalk talks back in the way that chalk has always communicated, by dreams and fossil encryptions and the sly subversion of everything I thought was solid in this world.

On top, I cannot see the route I have taken. Mist has rolled in, a titanium oxide full of the sea's breath, but already the sun is burning it away, thinning it to milk-in-water, to a fine infiltration, to nothing, and the sky that was crematorium bonemeal, thousands of plastic urns-worth of ash, is clear again. So many used to seek this summit. There are fifty miles of the world to observe, another coast and another country. To the east is Cwm Befos, a valley named after the Norman knight once lost for three days in these dunes, driven mad by the barracking hordes of great bush crickets (*Tettigonia vindissima*) occasionally still found here. I once held one in my hand: a little green warhorse in its chainmail.

Now a buzzard perches in de Bevos's place, a twice-booted, cappuccino-coloured buzzard, cowering from crows. Beyond the sea is Exmoor. Some days, I have counted every hedge and windscreen on that brow. But what's the outlook from England? On this side stand bureaucracy's towers of famine. Then Port Talbot's sprocketing flames as our poisons are incinerated. For a person from Porlock directly opposite Porthcawl the view is of the death throes of our industrial monotheism – an apocalypse's afterglow. And a sky full of scarlet macaws.

But these days few bother to climb. A brown sister, nervous as a wren; boys with a traffic bollard filled with beer; and a student with an Apple laptop, who turns the pool of its screen orange, then blue, two butterflies around her head, and the ibook drawling back to her in Californian, another voice out of the dune, so many lost in its galleries and down its corridors. I put my ear to the chalk and listen to the voices. Soon I will join them. Because there is no end to the languages wired under this sand or dancing about our heads.

The student writes. Into her lists she adds new words, for she is the latest discoverer of this place and therefore stands at the summit of all the other discoverers. There is so much here she never thought could be. Or would be. But in the chalk she is learning of the should be. Everything here has its appointed time and place. It is no accident she sits here. This is her day.

For now the writings are revealed. Some are left by earth, some by fire. Here are shell imprints from a tropical sea dead before metal was worked, for these too helped build this dune. Here are the squinancywort flowers which had gone to dust and are every year restored in Cwm Befos, white-pink-white on the summit track where atomic signatures are disregarded yet leap into the light, this crematorium of corals still cooling after millennia, still warm underfoot.

And as the sun climbs, everything alive this morning on the sulphur-smelling crest cranes to its azimuth – even for a moment this student in her headscarf with forefinger quieted on the keys and Latin covering her tablet.

Antenna of the Race

AND WHAT DO POETS DO? he asks. These days?

What you mean? I say.

How do you spend your time?

Well, I teach... Most of the week. Creative writing... Ever heard of that?

No, he says. So poets are teachers?

Sort of...

Intriguing. But I have always thought the poet, described in ideal perfection, would bring the whole soul of man into activity.

Well, why not? I say. Then when I go home I do a bit on the web...

The web?

Do a bit on the site. It's been made for me.

And what does this entail?

I suppose I key in all the material I've got. Then I add the date that I redrafted it.

Fascinating.

It's great, I say. No editors, to tell you what to do. It's like publishing everything you ever wanted. And no worries about rejection, or hanging round the slush pile, in some publisher's in-tray.

Slush?

Lot of it about, I say.

And what else?

I suppose I check for hits... You know, count how many people have signed on to the site.

Are there many?

You bet... Lots of students, doing their degrees on my work. I read their comments. Then there's the readings. Sort of personal appearances. Always stacking up.

What about the imagination?

What about it? I say.

Isn't it true that the poet diffuses a tone and spirit of unity, that blends and, as it were, fuses, each into each, by that synthetic and magical power, to which we have exclusively appropriated the name 'imagination'?

You never know, I say.

And that his power, first put into action by the will and understanding, and retained under their irremissive, though gentle and unnoticed control reveals itself in the balance or reconciliation of opposite or discordant qualities?

Could be... But all I say to my students, is show don't tell.

Show? Ah ha. I see your strategy. Of sameness, with difference; or the general, with the concrete; the idea, with the image; the individual, with the representative; the sense of novelty and freshness, with old and familiar objects; a more than usual state of emotion, with more than usual order; judgement ever awake, and steady self-possession, with enthusiasm and feeling profound and vehement.

Sounds like you're catching on, I say.

What are you presently reading, he asks?

Hold on, I say. Reading? That's bad news.

Indeed?

Influences, I say. They infect your style. Corrupt you.

Yes, he says. I had never thought of that.

Reading other writers is a dangerous, like, thing.

You don't read other writers?

You must be joking... Could be fatal to someone like me. Style's like gold dust...

Your very essence.

It's the meal ticket...

Your very soul.

The whole career.

Your genius.

That's very kind of you to say so, I say.

Yes, genius, he says. Like a green field reflected in a calm and perfectly transparent lake, the image is distinguished from the reality only by its greater softness and lustre. Like the moisture of the polish on a pebble, genius neither distorts nor false-colours its objects; but on the contrary brings out many a vein and tint, which escape the eye of common observation, thus raising to the rank of gems what had often been kicked away by the hurrying foot of the traveller on the dusty high road of custom.

Hey, now don't go over the top, I say. That kind of bollocks could give us all a bad name.

(With apologies to Samuel Taylor Coleridge.)

Skunk Hour

IT IS FAT AND AUSTERELY handsome. It is printed in three languages. It is, on the publisher's part, an undoubted labour of love. And it may prove for the same party a ruinous investment.

The volume is *In Een Ander Licht,* an anthology of twelve writers from Wales, brought out by Dutch publisher Wagner and Van Santen of Dordrecht. I am the book's editor. It is my job to help organise its Amsterdam launch. And of course it is up to me to assist with sales.

So this is my pitch. I walk with a box of books past the condomeries and the live fucking at the Casa Rossa, the sucking sessions and virtual orgies, past the girls in their aquariums, drowning before my eyes here in the dark of the Dam, the night already black as canal water, drowning sure to God with smiles on their faces and not a trace of the boredom, the terror I thought they were supposed to feel.

Feel? Feeling is finished here. Feeling vanished a long time ago. For feeling is not part of the agenda of these men in black, always in black, heads shaved, shoulders yoked thick by the gymnasium nautilus, the fat ones trailing behind, always behind. Sell poetry here? Well I'm trying. Here where the punters want pizza and strawberryflavour lickapussy and a head full of Heineken. It might be easier to be a puritan here. In fact, I sense my own puritanism growing effortlessly erect as I patrol the gwlis and ginnels around the canals. It might be easier to consider these neon streets as the corridors of a presbytery. It might be easier to act the apocalyptic, hollering doom.

But under my arm are Gwyneth Lewis's 'Oxford Booklicker' and Duncan Bush's 'East Side Story'. Such poems are acquainted with pornography in their own ways, but maybe with curiouser or kinder perversions than those on offer here in the Walletjes. Sell poetry? Yes, I'm trying. But it's the hardest job on the planet.

Sell poetry? The world doesn't want it. It has rarely wanted poetry. A pity really. *In Een Ander Licht* contains some marvellous writing.

At 3.30am I return to the hotel with my books. British psyche-delia seeps through the walls. Nothing has changed in thirty years except the marijuana menu: Super Skunk; White Widow; while Pink Floyd's back catalogue is exactly the same. The lunatic is on the grass, then in Roger Waters's head. And, as ever, the ashen faced flower of Aachen and Omskirk are staring into their Amstel, exhausted by their adventures in consciousness-changing, the debris of their eucharist covering the tables. Super Skunk? Guaranteed paranoid psychosis with an oblivion chaser.

I sniff the stoned room. Its air is the damask of dopesmoke. Poetry could live here, I have no doubt. There is nothing here that poetry has not already celebrated or subverted. So I take a table and open the book, to Bobi Jones reading in a rocking chair, feeling the tree sap alive in his chair's capillaries, the tree sap a waterfall that rises upwards, the sap itself an invisible tree blossoming here in the bar.

The words are waiting, ladies and gentlemen, you of the leaden lids, of the smoked out dreams, you, the self-proclaimed adventurers in what it means to be alive.

The Blue Wolf

A statutory man
in a Mercedes with a special licence plate
left without deciphering
the code of the third language. He was mute.
Because too many people
for the first time in life
were really speaking.
          Miroslav Holub, 'The Third Language'

SUDDENLY THE LILAC IS OUT. Then the white acer. A waiter moves across the square with a tray of Staropramen, the foam flying. On Prague's Charles Bridge the tourists stand listening to a violinist. They watch each other watching him. Is there anyone, I think, like the Czechs for bringing melancholy out of music? The sweetness that tastes of desperation. Revealing what was always there.

I hadn't been in Prague for years. Now I was unsure what I might find. Previously I had stayed on Jaicovsky Street and eaten in the workers' caff across the way. Rice and tripe. Monochrome food in a city remaking itself in technicolor. Already there were many Americans with their literary magazines and dreams of a Left Bank in what had been the Eastern Bloc.

But there was also uncertainty, and shabby people in the buffets drinking local cola and eating red wurst. And smoking. Everybody smoking. Yet no matter how miserable they had looked, they were real people. And now people are still smoking, they are differently miserable, but it is the anniversary of the changes, and of the end of the last restrictions on writers. Also, it is the anniversary of the death of Miroslav Holub, who had lived to know his poetry routinely described as great modern European verse. He had also seen Prague's Czech personality become more broadly European, immediately attractive to the young of the EU who have flocked to its squares. Intrigued by its history – mediaeval, baroque, art deco, totalitarian – their backpacks help build its future. Nothing there that Holub would not have expected. From both his poetry and his science – he was an immunologist – he understood that the system that silenced him was doomed. That his country, like his art, could not remain immune to the fevers of American or pan-European culture.

I often have difficulties with Holub's work. There must, I think, be something I am not reading. That something might be its music, its awareness of traditions, of literatures more profoundly rooted than the freewheeling verse forms and open spaces of US writing that would seem to influence him. Surely their prosody and scale are reactions to topographical immensities alien to Bohemia and wooded Moravia? Alien to people who must deal with statutory men? For sometimes Holub is loose or prosy as the Beats. His encodements are lost. Sometimes he doesn't make sense. But making sense in a totalitarian state makes no sense. And real sense could only be achieved in the third language.

In Prague since 1945 it has been paramount to think about a 'third language'. But this language is vital everywhere. Holub's first two languages are noted in the poem. They are Czech and Slovakian. Once it might have been as straightforward to define the third language. It is (is it not?): the language of the freedom of dissent. Or the secret language of the imagination? Or the language of individual identity? It could not be Russian, or German. But maybe English? Maybe not. For Holub the expert on immunities, the believer in the absolutism of scientific truth, it was the one language that could never be betrayed. After all, science would seem incorruptible, even by dictatorship. In the poem, Holub tells us that in the third language:

> oxygen was oxygen
> and a conic section passed through a fixed point
> and intersected a fixed line.

Chemistry and mathematics are irrefutable. Art can lie. Poets lied under the communist regimes of Czechoslovakia. But oxygen is oxygen. Science cannot lie. Therefore it is the truth. Holub tells us the people getting ready to speak the third language came from everywhere "[but] went one way, equal to themselves, / identified with one another, / like stem cells from the bone marrow / of the idea."

This language baffles authoritarianism.

So who are Holub's people, the ones who will speak the third language? They emerge from holes, from houses, from fly-ash, from hot water, from burning trees. But their real genesis is a revolution of the head: "And so it happened / That something like a disinherited idea / thought people up."

Something like a disinherited idea. A disinherited idea? It has taken me a long time to register what that means. There are disinherited ideas everywhere. But not everywhere do they think people up. Czech and Slovakian have their speakers, but it is the third language that counts. Maybe more importantly now than we realise.

For the statutory men were thwarted but not destroyed. They still cruise in their Mercedes. And perhaps science is not as truthful as it seemed. People are never uniform cells, no matter how rich the marrow of their propagation.

But suddenly it is dark in the square. A woman steps out of a doorway. Her jewels are the sparks of a midnight tram. Two men with shaven heads lean together over a cigarette. On the architrave above, a blue wolf in the plaster leaps between them.

Mi Buenos Aires Querido

Verano Porteño

The perspex that separates the football pitch of La Bombonera from the hordes is cracked and dull. Without it, the spectators could embrace the heroes of Boca Juniors whenever they cross the touchline. Crowds here comprise kids and dockworkers, fixers and hustlers, artists, pimps, ships' painters, chandlers, McDonald's burger flippers from up at Recoleta, in short, the real *porteños*, the proletariat of the river, the inhabitants and habitués of the barrio of Boca. And when their team plays River Plate the police put snipers on the stadium roof. Just in case those traditional rivalries take a turn for the worse.

God of Boca is Diego Maradona. Born in its docks, he's these days a little inflated. In fact, he looks like a wine-bottle-shaped palo borracho tree. And though now he lives in Cuba, his face is all over Buenos Aires in one hilariously demeaning sponsorship deal after another. (Unsurprising. He owes the Italian Football Federation eighteen million sterling in back taxes. Now that's style.) And such a face. Ignore its exhaustion's white-out. Appearances, they say, are deceptive. Even the crow sits on a green egg. So here's the vulpine cherub and the chopsy shoeshine boy: Maradona is both of these. Maradona is also the coke-dealer, the subway beggar, the ambassador. Maradona is genially priapic. Maradona even writes poetry. Of course Maradona writes poetry. Poetry is life and that's Maradona's game. Today Maradona is the global *porteño*, glad-handing Castro, god-handling the English, perplexing the press with his dialect, a species of *Boca lunfardo*. Here stands Diego Maradona. In the sniper's eye.

Adios Nonino

Outside the Casa Rosada the palm trees were burned by rioters trying to disperse tear-gas. So now their lianas are black as ancient ironwork. But the disappeared are still the disappeared. Even their outlines chalked on the plaza have faded from the cobbles, like their faces from their mothers' minds. The mothers are here again today. But they are here every day. With their gossip and cups of *mate*. With their knitting. It's quite the teaparty in the death zone.

But they are resolute. Sometimes they write on the ground.

No Somos Nada they write. Or *romper il silencio*. Which is ungrammatical but makes a point. Until the state confesses what it did with their children, the mothers will continue to congregate. Once they inhabited the zone of hope. Then the zone of grief. And then anger. Today it's the terrible zone of nothingness they find themselves within. Or maybe it's not so terrible. They're cheerful enough, sifting the black leaves for the last of the *mate* juice, strong as tobacco. Anyway, it's no big secret. Everybody knows what happened. Everybody knows where the children are. After a while the mind will heal itself as best it can. It will put itself back together like a broken glass. And admit the day's dislocated light.

Mi Buenos Aires Querido

It's a hot winter's day in Old Palermo. The jacaranda is stripped, the air blowing out of the Subte like a hairdryer. As usual, weird weather. In Buenos Aires, it should be the cusp of winter and spring. Instead, here's an urban summer's day squatting in the calendar. A summer's day when the sourmilk smell of a new continent attaches itself to me. Or my own sourmilk aroma seeps ahead of me into the Plaza de Mayo.

Buenos Aires has a corrosive vitality. This is heightened by the daily demonstrations about agriculture, the death of the provinces, the disappeared. But chiefly, these days, the demos concern money. Here's Banco Galicia in its baroque fortress. Here's HSBC daubed with *lunfardo* grafitti.

Chorros says the graffiti. Thieves. A spittle-filled word out of BA's urban Castellano, a street dialect effortlessly adapting to whatever modern horror is thrown at it. During one centro-wide protest I walk in a tickertape squall towards Defensa.

Hey, Heavyballs, someone says as the paper drifts down from

the offices. Gorra fag?

That's *lunfardo*. The lingo here. And camped beside HSBC the people share cigarettes and hotdogs, while inside the vault the peso decays like a radioactive isotope. Spreading its plague.

Taquito Militar

Here, before me, the choreography of rape. The men, the women, all are dancers. The men dancers rape the women. The women dancers give birth. Their babies start to grow. The men rape the children. The process becomes a historical continuum. Then the women die. The children die. After a while there is no-one left to assault. Bored, the men rape each other. They snarl into one another's flesh. There can be only one outcome. Soon they have killed themselves. The play ends in gibberish and an electronic cacophony. Before the lights were turned off a woman stood quivering before me, her pelvis a dinner plate with blue cracks in the glaze. Even her scream had been stolen from her. Who was she? A ghost from a sexual concentration camp, a girl on an errand, picked off the street and institutionalised in purgatory? Nun, student, someone who offended *argentinidad*? How did such people vanish? Black as swifts they plummeted from helicopters above the Rio de la Plata and fell into a history that still refuses to be written.

These actors represent the disappeared and their disappearers. They are characters in *Memoria (20 Anos de Investigacion)* staged by Grupo Teatro Libre. Tonight is the first part of a trilogy by Omar Pacheco, but I've no wish to see the other installments. There are only fifteen of us here in the blackness, waiting for the lights to come up. Maybe the woman is still in front of me. It's impossible to tell. There is no music and no applause. Drama like this is dangerous in Buenos Aires. The policeman in his leathers, the keeper of the kiosko, where were they twenty years ago? But maybe Argentina is trying to come to terms with itself and its Dirty War. Last night, I sat in the paradise seats at the Teatro Colon. The opera was *In Bluebeard's Castle*. Bella Bartok, too, exposed our evil. His chords dragged like prison chains. How I ground my teeth under the gold leaf. Below me, the capital's aristocracy leapt to applaud.

El Choclo

In Buenos Aires there's surprisingly little animosity towards the Welsh, those bristling little Britishers. After the World Cup defeat by England, the journal *Ole*'s headline was a three inch high "Fuck You, Beckham." It was withdrawn and is now a collector's item. I sought everywhere for a copy. And once, my daughter had a pizza delivered with the word *puta* arranged in olives. Meanwhile, around the dockland development of Puerto Madero, the old iron capstans have been preserved. Each boasts the maker's legend: Global Foundry Company, Cardiff. Ah, such was our heyday in the flood.

El Dia Que Me Quieras

In the café I drink a bottle of champagne. This is the café where Jean Luis Borges would push his black knight around the board. Somehow I always think of Borges playing black. And making knight moves. No piece builds a labyrinth like the knight. No sacrifice is like a knight's sacrifice. It's instructive for a writer to read Borges. I can almost feel his twinkling dismissal as a life's work is cast, admittedly with most other literature, onto his bonfire of the inanities.

Now fittingly, it's time to visit the city of tombs. Death's barrio.

In the raindark ginnels of the mausoleum garden, Evita lies with the bankers and the generals. But Borges isn't here. In fact, it's impossible for me to consider Borges dead. Instead, I picture a plasterbroken stairwell, a doorknob with a serpent's face. There he is, at the rolltop desk. That's Borges, surely, that figure in the corner of the room, doodling labyrinth within labyrinth with his black knight and discovering there is no minotaur in the maze but man himself, a man who has let go the thread and been waiting for us to discover him. A man who looks a little like...

By 3pm it's dusk in the catacombs. The bones and ribbons are indistinct in the glass coffins. But the present generation, the young, who should bring flowers, keeps well away as the dead implode in their palaces. Maybe the young too are drinking champagne. It's cheap enough. Maybe they are toasting these magnificently deceased moguls of Buenos Aires who now must spill together like the jacaranda leaves under this armorial rain.

Me Da Pena Confesarlo

Earlier in the week we'd tried the Spanish Club for one of those lunches where midday metamorphoses into early evening. Crisis or not, it was full. Ancient couples toasted each other. For what? For surviving. Naturally. For outliving the tyranny and the terror and getting away with the pearls unpawned and the Miami deposit account's bottom line intact. Liveried waiters breezed past. There were suckling pigs roasted gold. I looked at their sad snouts and considered my vow.

Three days later we are in Las Canitas.

Si, morcilla, the Maitre D. says.

I translate. Christ, he means blood pudding. There's also an assortment of ribs and *bife de chorizo* everywhere in this top room of the restaurant, hanks, shanks and pink concertinas of meat, all visible in a kitchen full of hilarious girls. A chef in check trousers waves a cutlass.

Not that I'm squeamish. I used to eat this stuff, this black pudding, marbled with fat. The night sky, I thought as a child at Sunday morning breakfasts, my star-atlas open in the bedroom, how like a June midnight sky were the bubbling rings of blood scraped out of the pan and on to my plate. And the burned bits best. My grandfather used to bring it on a bike along with mint, *rhiwbob*, American cream soda. All the exotica.

I've since been a vegetarian for thirty years, yet this feast is inescapable. The Quilmes is arriving and here comes a malbec the colour of snapdragons. These are drinks to make a man relish meat, not to mention sinew and intestine, to convert any cud-loving vegan into Dionysus's disciple.

Outside between shifts, the tango couples play chess. Rabbits and deer are racked in dainty crucifixions along the street. Try it all, I say. Forget *la cuenta*. Instead, order the *udre*, the *chinchulines*. Look what those succulents did for Manuel Puig's prose and Batistuta's footwork. Because I have a peso bundle in my pocket which I'm not going to convert. And all that cash is slated for this *parrillada*.

Yes, money. What a drag. Today I cowered in a taxi while the driver examined the banknotes I offered.

Falso, he said of the first.

Then *falso, falso, falso*, as he peered at the others. Indisputably duds. And an egregious batch. Not that I could really tell. But he sniffed at me as if the counterfeiter's perfume still hung in my sleeves.

So pity the poor peso. It's a ghost of itself. The banks are full of ghosts, and outside are the haunted middle classes who have seen their futures mutate. They even burn the palm trees in front of the Casa Rosada. But nothing helps. The currency disguises itself with name changes but Argentinian inflation seems as ineradicable as malaria. Once you have it, you have it all: the night sweats, the grotesque fears. So the protestors swarm into the suburbs and take their delirium with them. It proves contagious.

On that bike my grandfather used to cycle up Heol Eglwys. Then it was the only street in the village, and until the miners' strike of 1921 had been an avenue of elms. But hungry families needed the wood and now there is no-one left who understands what those trees meant. So how can I remember trees I've never seen? But I do. I was born in their branches and they grow in my soul. Trees are family. So tomorrow for the last time I will stand under the palms, a penitent and a pilgrim. Those are the palms Borges sat beneath, and where the chalk outlines of disappeared students are drawn. Now they're black as the chainwork of the widows' cages in the Teatro Colon. But take a vow-breaker's word for it. Soon there'll be green amongst their scorched scales.

Adios Muchachos (Septiembre 6, 2027)

The past. They say it's a different country. Where we're all asylum seekers. Now it's midnight at the Bar Sur in San Telmo. I've been to church today and thought, as I always do, how the pillars of the altars resemble an engine's pistons trembling beneath the finger-tips of those who dare touch. In the gloom I thought I might glimpse the sparking of faith's combustion. But it's too late for that. Now outside there is rain on the cobbles and the poor are sifting rubbish. A junta arrived. A junta was removed. Bodies fell from the helicopters but La Plata is broad and dark and no-one heard the cries. In a corner I sit with my malbec. So here I am, the thin white duke of tango, tuxed to the teeth, the carnation behind my ear the colour of driftwood.

Some things comfort. Above me in the wainscoting my last partner's stiletto still quivers when a train passes. Such a blade. Kicked off in her grief. How she held me upon her thighs, her gaze exhausting mine, her tears remarkable, like the little firelit emeralds in her chemise. She vanished, as they all do, one night at the Bar Sur, the bar where only one survivor remains to listen to the long white notes, the brief black. An institution they say, the Bar Sur. Now a camera flashes and the *bandoneon* sighs. My last tango will take place here. I who have danced the city through. Every pose a sculpture. A sculpture of a second. Every tango a room of sculptures. And every step a persona. So who was I? The lover? The impostor? All of those. The soldier with his hissing crop? As if you couldn't guess. And here I sit, having seen it all and remembering almost nothing. Yes, the tyranny of remembering. I have overthrown that regime. Such a blessing. Some battles, you see, can be won. Now all I have in my eyes is the stain on her teeth, her teeth black with malbec, blacker than blackberries, blacker than shiraz that malbec black, and the candlelight back and forth between the walls of the room, and all I have in my ears is the sound she makes when she crosses her black legs, the sound of her thighs that are licked by candlelight, the tiny rustling sound that a blackbird makes when it opens its wings and rises from its nest.

The Ruby

IT'S CHILLY, BUT I SIT OUTSIDE. The garden lies between
tenement walls that protect it from winds off the East River.
Cherry leaves drift down, but the sassafras clings on and I sit in
what shade it offers and wait. Next door's oranges drop over the
wall, little balls that run under this table, bitter candies. From the
beds the pokeweed stares at me with its Romanian eyes. Now, if I
can make myself small enough he might come this morning. This
morning of all mornings. If I can still the thunder of my pulse.

Last night the clocks went back an hour. When I awoke today I
turned my watch to the past. This is the hour I will live twice, a
morning hour in a garden of official winter. Last night I took a
wineglass of Abbey Ale brewed up the road behind the Turkey's
Nest saloon. A free nightcap, the counterboy said, a ruby of sleep.
Ah, and such sleep, dreamless and crimson as the measured beer.
So here out of the gift of sleep is another gift, a gift of time, the
best gift any man might have. And I use it by watching the cherry
leaves and the sassafras, knowing he will come soon, if I am patient
enough, if I am quiet under the trees, this table before me glazed
with candlewax and my coffee asmoke in the cold.

Big minutes pass. Out in McCarren Park the kids are in their
hooded parkas as if celebrating winter, acolytes of the new season
these disciples of the cold, kids who hit baseballs in the bullpens
while this Sunday like every Sunday the alarm drones on the wall
of the School of Automotive Trades, the alarm that will ring all
through this extra hour, its red beam pacing to and fro in its cage
on the wall. In D & D men with grey skin rummage in bins of
Mexican underwear, in Christina's a woman sits at the counter
making a pile of pennies that will pay for her perogies and thimble
of applesauce, the day coming alive in this extra hour, each of us
using it as we think best, aware this hour is a gift that cannot be
refused, the trains running under our feet, the trains under this
garden come whispering from the hollows of the world, the

Nassau, the Greenpoint trains, people flooding into those subterranean halls where a fiddler plays a gypsy tune older than this city, the city coming alive around me, the Polish language sizzling like a miner's phlegm on the sidewalk, those Brooklyn Poles getting ready for Polish weather, the menfolk picking socks out of the bargain bins, grey men with blue eyes, and in Christina's the coffee black in its bulb, the girls in their booth who share a cherrysoda through their extra hour while Christina herself in immaculate uniform stirs up the cauldron of soup, another hour for soup, a soup she has served us for these thousands of years.

Perhaps I had expected his Audubon image. Grey kingfisher, exotic and aloof, a princeling in a polished cuirass. I sit so quiet I can hear the cacophony across the river, the Empire State straight ahead lit like a candle, silver this morning, green last night, nosecone already ringed with mountaineers. I sit so still I can hear my blood shuttling on its loom and then the roadcrew drilling on Manhattan Avenue but now I know the mockingbird was here all the time.

The extra hour is passing. But I suspect there is another hour after the extra hour. I also suspect that there will be a calling to account as to how I use this extra hour and the extra hour after that. Yes, a reckoning. Last night, my life ended. I picked up the ruby and held it to the light. Such a stone. The greatest weight I had ever borne. Such a draught. I drained the wineglass and fell into a fairybook slumber. And awoke in this garden at a table on which I have pricked a name in candlewax.

Soon I too will sip Christina's borsht and rummage for Panamanian workshirts with men short of vitamin D. Outside I can hear the marathon runners, pounding this hour up from the Verrazano Bridge, coming out of Lafayette and kicking through the coffee lids that spin in the breeze, cracking the locust tree pods blown from Guernsey Street. Because the day is coming to the boil. Morning doves cross the square of sky above, and the sky that was grey and then blue is grey again and the extra hour has gone but here's another arrived as I knew it would, and the name I have written gleams white in the wax and I know that even if I stay here until the oranges become ghost oranges and roll like spectres about my feet that there will be another hour to be reckoned and then another awaiting its reckoning.

So the hours pass and I wait for the Brooklyn mockingbird, the king of all backyard birds, little wisecracker in his striped parka, dealing tickets for the Subway Series, Yankees, Mets, the city can't lose, a wiseguy barking on about the impossibility of making a sensible bet on the Marathon as the last runners go by in the cold and the drinkers out of the Turkey's Nest cheer them on, those lame suckers still running, cheer the runners who run through extra hour after hour before those drinkers who drank through their own extra hour duck back into the warmth and tavern light, their street corner saloon that has stood through a hundred years of extra hours. Then I uncoil myself from under the leaves and looking back see the shape of myself burnt into the air before the night seals it in a perfect graft, while the mockingbird with the moon in his eye rises from the branch and says what he has to say.

The Allotment

MY SPADE'S A SABRE in this earth. It cuts through the soil's silk, so dry, so fine, and after three days the plot is dug. This field was given by St John the Baptist's to the poor of Newton-Nottage, that they might grow vegetables and not go hungry. Not poor, not hungry, I am digging my allotted eight perches' worth of church land, digging where generations of diggers have dug, turning up Bronze Age brooches, Roman amulets, buttons and shards, all of which I wash and keep in a glass vase, because in this garden on the duneland edge, with its limestone charnels, its Range Rovers stacked with woad-tipped hoes, is history. Nor am I out of it.

I sweat the good sweat. A swan goes over, neck long as the flag-pole on St John's. Digging is dreamwork, I decide. Its physical rhythm frees the mind. Soil's our surety yet nothing's more surreal than its carnival animals under a surplice of sorrel.

So on the imagination's allotment the sand is loosed and I'm returned to the day before yesterday. In the Jardin des Plantes the ostriches were sitting in the rain. They looked like little black and white hayricks. The tropical house was shut. Evening had come and the keepers were pouring the wine of the jaguars back into the night. So whose were those? Those snail-tongs, that snail-fork? Poor snails. That glimpsed too late the perils of parsley butter. And whose was that carafe of violet Bergerac? And whose bread? Whose money? Whose life?

Mine it appears. Though most things these days reveal them-selves as dreams. Thirty-five years ago I walked with Biffer Jenkins through what as then the market town of Bridgend. We did it French style, arm-in-arm. How mortified was Bridgend. But Biffer held on tight, speaking of cafés that served liquorice and lemon-ade, of railway stations where the guards were post-impressionists and the conveniences green and weedy lilyponds. Biffer evoked light that would make catechumens of us all in a religion of light. For Biffer Jenkins, Parisian light was an article of faith. Ah Biffer, that walk. An epoch shone in its oils. But I was the snail that would not be winkled out.

The day before yesterday I had nothing in mind but avoiding the rain. So I ducked into the Musée Carnavalet. Five minutes later, there was René Crevel. Or rather René Crevel captured by the artist Jaques-Emile Blanche. A corner portrait. Here, I swore, was the essence of the man, the youthful arrogance, the turmoil. Crevel looked to be putting on a brave face in a crisis.

Born in 1900, Crevel was inevitably appalled by the First World War. Like many of the Surrealist group, he could see what else was coming. I stood by his portrait and peered into his torment. How he squirmed in his excellent clothes. Here was a man whose books, theoretically, are available from Wal Mart. Would that be good or bad for a surrealist?

Crevel "will be read more and more as the wind carries away the ashes of the 'great names' that preceded him," wrote Ezra Pound. "If you don't find Crevel's fever contagious, then you are definitely vaccinated against rebellion," says another admirer.

But the rain was not a dream. On Rue de Rivoli it became torrential. At C&A's the doors were tied shut with parcel tape. Workers were picketing the entrances and the shop was closed. Why does this seem extraordinary? Because workers lost the war ages ago. To see workers oppose their employers is now rare. Global capital has triumphed and workers work. Or snivel and skive. But fight back? Draft a manifesto? Here was a turn-up.

I was getting soaked. Opposite C&A's is number 59. Something was happening there too. I walked in and was greeted. Here was a six storey mansion. On the first floor were artists cooking, sleeping, making art. Come in and see the mess the imagination makes. Every room, and there were scores, was a studio. The air was scorched by oxy, floors littered with shock absorbers and tailors' dummies. Slowly, I ascended.

All of 59 Rue de Rivoli was occupied by artists. Good, bad, how they abounded. And soon I was at the top beneath a yellow skylight. Under the rain the room was an aquarium. A note was pinned there:

Arretez de prendre des photos
Prenez les temps
de regarder

Amongst the squat-psychos, the apprentices and the miracle makers, René Crevel might have found something to admire at 59 Rue de Rivoli. Commerce well knows it would make a gorgeous Gap or middling software company's Parisian HQ. So the artists in their honeycomb are literally under siege. Which is how they might perform best. But poor Crevel. Whatever was offered by writing or hypnosis and its loam of surrealist sleep could not overcome meaninglessness.

Did he dig? Because, yes, digging is dreamwork. Leaning like a beanstick I'm spellbound by speedwell, little blue Veronica whose root runs where it will. Over my gilded tilth. The spade goes in. It goes in. Now I am steadfast. Now I am earthed. I am the steward. This is my stipend. I am one who stands beneath an eight hundred year-old church with its own rebellious art and exhortations on self-help for the starvelings of our parish. Grow your own food, I say. It's a revolutionary act.

Had your lockjaw jab? asks a friend.

Thinking about it, I reply.

But here's to you, René Crevel, who in 1935 performed the surrealist's ultimate act. By then it was only too plain what was coming. While today it's still the day before yesterday. I turn the earth, lift the carafe, tear the bread.

Oh pale snail pardon my pitchfork.

Baseball

I WONDER WHAT IT IS I have to say to you. About where I am from and what you would make of it. And what you will write down in your notebook, if you use such a thing. There's always an answer to questions like that.

The room is lit by one bulb. One lamp like a mallow on the edge of night. I sit on the sofa with my coat on my knees and look at the light. And wonder what it is I have to say to you.

The light is the colour of those sweets, purple hearts, or love hearts, mauve I suppose. There's always an answer to questions like that: one lamp like a mallow on the edge of night.

Out in the yard you are playing with the girl. Earlier, she'd been running around the trees, as I wondered what it was I had to say to you, those two trees, the cherry and the mock-orange, the two trees in that midtown garden that grow together straight up between the walls. The room is lit by one bulb.

She often did that, you had said, a fierce little thing, talking to the trees as if they were her friends, one lamp like a mallow on the edge of night. I never doubted it.

A child of eight with rings under her eyes. And I wonder what it was I have to say to you. She comes every week, that fierce little thing. I can see those rings like two love hearts thumbed up from the packet outside the Penyrheol sweetshop. The room is lit by one bulb. But she seems happy enough. There's always an answer to questions like that.

And a mockingbird you say, that will sit in the mock-orange. I never doubted it. Even sometimes a bluebird, there on Twenty Second Street, a bluebird in the cherry, ready for a sleepover. And I wonder what it is I have to say to you. And what you will write in your notebook if you use such a thing.

There's always an answer to questions like that. I think you mean it is a real garden, out there, between the offices. I never doubted it. The mockingbird will sound like a mockingbird; the cherry lose its leaves, a bluebird sit in the cherry, ready for a sleep-over. And you charge only half price for the girl. The room is lit by one bulb, one lamp like a mallow on the edge of night.

Now you start with the game, throwing her the baseball, the skipping rope left hanging from a branch. And I wonder what it is I have to say to you. The girl is hitting the ball against the trees, against the walls, a fierce little thing, lobbing it through the branches and against the glass where the love heart shines in the daylight. The room is lit by one bulb. One lamp like a mallow on the edge of night.

Half price for baseball, you say. I never doubted it. But I don't ask if it will be better if the child plays with her mother or father. In their own yard. There's always an answer to questions like that. Instead, I wonder what it is I have to say to you. The room is lit by one bulb

You throw the yellow plastic baseball and she strikes it with the blue plastic baseball bat. I can see how seriously she is taking it, that fierce little thing. As I wonder what it is I have to say to you.

And there you are under the mock-orange, and that little girl is over her time but you are still throwing the ball and she is still hitting it at the glass, straight at me on the sofa, my coat on my knees, where one lamp like a mallow flowers at the edge of night. And I wonder what it is I have to say to you, and what you will write down in your notebook if you use such a thing. There's always an answer to questions like that.

Coal

COAL

I distrust that word. What does it imply but subterranean suffocation? Working-class claustrophobia? A culture with the roof fallen in? In the museums, fragments of a forgotten language are pieced together, an effort made to understand a cataclysm. But I learn it's rarely like that in the coalfield. For here I am at the HQ gate of National Coal Board Area Number 2 escorting my mother around the ruins.

Not that there are ruins to see. We are not into ruins anymore. But at Area Number 2 there's not a sign to tell the visitor what this place meant to the world. There's not a plaque, not a brick upon another brick to indicate how this nothingness in its time controlled the lives of hundreds of thousands of people. Only a gate that leads to a wood of spectral buddleia.

The offices where my mother typed her coal chores on a ribboned Remington, where she looked up and saw for the first time the thin man from Rangoon, my father, at his own coal chores, are demolished. If you want to see absolute demolition, the sacrilege of sackage, go to Area Number 2. There's nothing there. Only a woman left to paint the air and hear the Remingtons ring.

But back then, everything was coal. The Fourteenth Army had returned from Burma, the emaciated subalterns and skin-and-bone corporals of the Welch Regiment were trying to fashion a life after Tungoo, after Mawchi. And demobbed legions, which included my father, entered the byzantium of coal that was Area Number 2.

Three hundred million years ago when Wales lay on the equator God decreed that this part of the world should one day provide coal. The geology was inescapable. Because geology is totalitarian no-one argued with it. With everything else we could have bent the rules: invoked character, nature, even genetics. But we couldn't argue with geology. Or with another geological force, the UK government, when it decreed coal must cease. But that proclamation came too late for me. I was already made. Made by coal. Coal made me when my mother looked up from her typewriter. Coal made me when my father, malarial, too small for his suit, a second hand Meakers of Piccadilly in West of England wools, followed the buyers down the National Coal Board corridor and into the typing pool. So there is coal in my blood. There is coal in my bones. I never think about it, but surely my heart is made of coal.

And now here are two of us on our visit to nowhere. The gate opens, the buddleia drips rain and there is a rain-washed nothing where the area headquarters used to be. A site of grim pillage. Two of us today, but I think of my father amongst the treeferns, sipping from pitcher plants, macheteing the mangroves. In three hundred million years there will be coal measures in Burma. In Myanma. God is decreeing it as I write. And there's no argument about that. Freedom fighters cannot win against geology. The Generals of Myanma cannot place geology under house arrest. Not even the Fourteenth Army, not even the Welch Regiment with its muletrains and genial headhunters scouting the way could defeat geology.

But at least my father had medals. Not that he kept them. Down the road in the munitions factory the girls turned yellow. They weren't given medals. Instead they went to the Palais de Danse and the Grand Pavilion, with unseasonal tans of saffron face-powder, in yellow nylons of dynamite dust.

No-one gave the colliers medals either. But how we've made up for it since. Now we award the miners literature's sympathy medals, art's nostalgia medals, the sentimental medals pinned on by politicians, by historians, by children who'll never need to squeeze themselves into the coffin-deep seams of Garth Ton Mawr or Pen Llwyn Gwent.

So what am I doing here? Here at the gate in the afternoon downpour. Asking for a medal of course. For a medal on the gate because there is nowhere else to put it now. A medal that records what has vanished. What has vanished as utterly as the treeferns and equatorial orchids that flourished where the buddleia now spills its rain. Because you cannot argue with geology. Or with the new geology. Because there is a new geology now. It's a speeded up geology. Three hundred million years in three hundred million seconds. It's that stratum of amnesia that is building itself, a buddleia leaf here, a memorial stanza there, between the now and the what's-to-come. That's the new geology. Open the gate at Area Number 2, off the Maesteg Road, in the village of Tondu, in the country of Wales, and watch its black seam laying itself down.

Learning to Swim

I'M ASLEEP AND AWAKE TOGETHER. Sleep is female and sleep is young. Sleep speaks Croatian although her words are never pronounced but appear in her eyes, which say *gavrilovic* and *cedivita*, because that's the language of sleep. It's all her lullaby, all that nonesuch's neon nonsense, and where I stand under the cathedral the trams pass on the wet rail and I dream of a language itself asleep.

Late autumn and the sea is warm. The Welsh seas are warmer than for decades. So fifty years late I'm learning to swim. The high pressure swells of August are still here, the waves high and overhead, their salt addictive, their power instructive.

The shore towards Sker is all needles and nibs, holding the ocean in a thousand razor-rimmed chalices. Every day at this spot on my way to the sands I christen myself at a limestone font. To cross these badlands I must balance on knifeblades. It's a tormented territory, as if a breaking wave had frozen in its splintering three hundred million years ago. Then there's a twenty foot cliff to shimmy down but already I'm starting to undress.

Now, how quickly come the thrillings. Though numberless, here are a selection.

To walk bareskinned across the sand.

To cross the laminarian frontier and feel the salt in your body speaking to the salt in the sea.

To encounter the shallows.

To float and face the surely unreachable land.

To sink into the waves' creamy karst while an octet of oystercatchers passes a metre overhead.

To hear the next wave's approach, its sucking and hurrumphing, and the dungeon floor drag of it advance.

Such a life. Surely those are elemental moments of true living.

★

"Europe will end in blood". That's what he says, over the Hotel Dubrovnik's coffee. I hold his gaze for three seconds but his eyes are too blue, his expression unremitting. Intimidating, yet oddly inanimate. At least his friend is not here, that bookish ideologue who last night would not suffer my arguments and laughed off any suggestion that the European Union is not run by freemasons, by Zionists, by UK bankers. Laughed off as idiocy all notions that the world is not shaped by conspirators; a cabal that any day will reveal itself and the extent of its malevolence.

If it joins the European Union, Croatia will be finished. That was one of these men's beliefs. Already Bavarians are motoring south in their limousines to colonise Istria, Italian second-home owners pricing Adriatic Croats out of their heritage.

But it's happening everywhere, I say. And now Croatia has independence. The world knows you exist, your red and white checks seen in every sports bar on this satellite TV planet.

Pretty patronising stuff. I should have kept my mouth shut. But my head was full of seawater and the hot labyrinth of Sker. Now here I was in Zagreb to give a paper on 'globalisation and literature', specifically on translating from a minority into a majority language (*the* majority language). Such translation made me more than a free radical of globalisation. I was a dangerous bacillus in the European bloodstream. Good for my blue-eyed colleague for not stating the obvious.

Two nights previously a group of us had sat in a midnight garden, watching Mars cross the southern sky. Zagreb was somewhere below, unseen but palpable, a radioactive city beneath its ridge. We ate aubergines spiced with pimentos, sipped black Macedonian wine.

Ah, poor Republika Makedonija, someone muttered. That country is no country. Its language is no language. And poor Macedonians. When they look to the west, what do they see? Albania. The insane Republika e Shqiperise. Where a family feud can last five hundred years. That is a Macedonian's western horizon. Some places are cursed. Macedonia is cursed, landlocked in its ligature of borders. Still, those Macedonians make good grog.

That too was an elemental moment. We all seemed to sense it.

The satire stopped and we concentrated on the Martian cabaret. For the war god was reborn golden as a buddha. We sipped and stared from the trees. The pimentos were sweet in my teeth, the night soothing with a warm October's currents and soon I was dreaming in my cell at the Dubrovnik. A bed, a chair, a writing desk. Perfect. And a window on the main square, a window filled with the twin steeples of the Cathedral of the Assumption of the Virgin Mary and Saint Stephen. Twin steeples lit like two black candles in my room. That was a room I would come to love.

"Why isn't Macedonia a country?" I asked. But there was nobody there. I was at the window and somehow it was 4.30am. The merchants in the square were preparing their stalls: a woman with a tray of chestnuts, a man carrying a sunflower taller than himself across the dark flags. And surely I was dreaming. I had floated through sleep hearing the waves' approach, the waves that lifted and overwhelmed. Mars was setting behind my eyes, but Zagreb was already bustling with gods, a god of trams and a god of chilis, and whether I was standing or not at the window I was still dreaming of the sea at Sker, its gwlis and beilis, the medieval town the sea had built, a warren of fissures between Gwter y Cŵn and Pwll Dafan, the sand raked in each cave to a screed of gemstones, the purple scrim of weed hung like wall tapestries, and all that limestone world ringing hollow with the tide out, the white lines of its sandbars scored along Scarweather four miles into the Channel. You must accept my word for this. There is no Rough Guide to these places. They are too real. But if you require a scout to take you to the skermongering sea we could go in our sleep. We would visit the cellars under the promontory where I might introduce you to cyclopian thieves, the hydras and hermaphrodites in their carnival, while the trams passed in that same sleep. Crossing sleep's border we would find ourselves in two places at once, because two places are what the god of sleep allows, and in the square below the advertising signs would be alive like a driftwood fire. *Krass* they might say, or *vartek*, or *foto materijal*, the tram passengers nodding awake as they are carried past on the wave, the cathedral angels weighing chilies on their market scales, the black chilies, the gold chilies, such baskets of chilis cathedral ikons all.

★

One day I slip out of the iron door of the writers' centre. I seem to float away from our conference. I visit the courtyard where the vulcaniser works. Soon I am at the fishmarket examining a dorado, then a shark's mouth open like a Brazilian geode. A woman stands over a sink of sardines like someone washing a chandelier. Most of the creatures are as alien as their names. Each fish wears an umlaut and a circumflex. These words trail fins and gills. These fish are extinct dialects. These words are oysters shocked from their shells. These are squamous words preserved in ice, words pulled from the Slavic reefs of the Adriatic's archipelagos. These are fish with famished vocabularies. In their refrigerators these fish look like the sounds of the languages to come.

I drift through the market. Nobody sees me. Maybe I am invisible. And I wonder again what a language dreams. A language anointed in sleep's soft toxin. In Zagreb I could almost visualise it. What I had glimpsed from the Dubrovnik's window was a language's dreaming face as the number 6 tram arrived with its bell ringing and I saw myself squeeze out with the students and headscarved women into consciousness. Whatever stop that is.

On our last day a feast is given in honour of the debaters of globalisation: kebabs burning on a sword; slivovitz. No angst here or scholars' abstractions. Academics are always hungry for something and they do the meal justice. But what had gone before was thin fare. Or, more correctly, too difficult for me. I am no literary or political theorist. Abstractions such as 'power' and 'beauty' poured from the translators' hutch, but I had no faith in them. Yet I'm prepared to think that globalisation will find its Charles Darwin. We already talk of the evolution of technological species. But faith? Another enormous word. Faith to me is as cavernous as a deserted airport, the carousels still going round. But I listened hard. If I was an impostor, so was everyone else. Some of the delegates were charlatans in five languages. And hadn't I been plucked unwilling from the sea, the sea that had been my home for weeks, the sea uniquely warm, its waves bronze with suspended sand and reddening from the west, my own sea that might never be as warm again in my lifetime.

Yes, that moment. I turned to the shore and saw how far the current had taken me. The beach was deserted. Gulls were seeking hermit crabs, the rock pools filled with Macedonian wine. What was it my mother told me once? Remember, you can drown in the shallows. Which is the irony of home. Slowly the waves were growing dark. The sky had become a succession of scarlet atolls. There was no-one watching and no-one waiting. Of that moment I was the only witness, riding the swell on a European shore, as behind me and before me in a hotel bar were and would be the blue-eyed men, shuffling their papers, whispering of the chaos that's to come.

The Angel

THERE'S A NEW HARLEY on a plinth. The counter is a varnished beam that runs into the dark of the club. On stage a famous jazzman plucks his bass. Around him the other musicians weave their own signatures, daring or votive, as they choose. Every so often a waiter appears and asks if we need more drinks. Meanwhile at the entrance, lean greeters, oiled like wrestlers, wait for the rush that never comes.

The club is new. So new that most of Budapest has never heard of it. It's located in what was an intimidating area, a dockside of unlit alleys. Stand outside and you hear the Danube slapping its waves against the wharf. But inside, for the twenty or so customers who have discovered the venue, what attracts are the smells of money, of the new world, and something other than money in this converted warehouse, something darker and sweeter and more dangerous, maybe something like the Danube itself, brushing its own rich cargoes over the walls of its prison outside.

As I'm an English speaker the staff are attentive. They speak their proud English to me, offering those English words which are so important now, showing off words which are more valuable than heroin, than diamonds. It's smugglers' lore. Trade in English and you cannot lose on the investment. Forget the euro, the dollar, the poor, besieged forint. English is the currency that should fill your pocket, fuel your life. Without it, you'll know poverty. Without it, my son, my daughter, you will not count.

The next day the river is free and carries the sky on its back. I follow it like a guide. But soon the horizon vanishes. Today is St. David's Day and now snow is falling. The street's orange globes grow dim as staff trudge to the consulates. On the riverbank all is dereliction. The Four Seasons is a palace of pigeons. Soon, inevitably, it will host EU trade delegations. But there is magnificence in that dereliction, magnificence that looms and gutters as the snow intensifies. On Szechny-lanchid the wind becomes too keen. So I turn up Jozsef Atila Street and in a café I read an English language weekly. The columns are filled with complaints about rap artists and heavy metal groups touring Hungary and leaving their debris of rap and heavy metal words in the minds of the young. English is out of control, say the writers. English is a blind giant stamping through a cornfield. Hungarian, meanwhile, has fifteen million speakers. Doomed, say the columnists. In the long run it's doomed.

Ah, that long run. Which none of us will finish. Where I was brought up my garden overlooked a chapel yard. Through the knotweed glinted a gravestone vocabulary. There was one word I always sought. And such a word. *Coffadwriaeth*. An angel guarded it, an angel with a marble book. But every year the angel bent lower, every year the knotweed was higher around its wings, its face. The knotweed was hollow and red-freckled. Red as the young trout in the Ffornwg. One year the word was completely hidden. Invisible to all but those who knew where to look. And surely I was the only one who knew that secret. There's an angel in the undergrowth, I said to myself. My friend who hides in the thicket. And guards a word.

I'm in Budapest to teach English. Or to encourage its use as a language for poetry. I am an ambassador, an emissary, an enemy. This morning I met a beggar halfway across the bridge. His body was crumpled like a ball of paper; tears had gouged his cheeks. Although I had money I didn't offer it. Instead I spoke to the man. I spoke to him in English. This evening I saw him again. He was drinking coffee with friends, laughing, his body straight. It's clearly a miracle. But that's what English can do. Miraculous English. And the beggar sipped his coffee and looked through me and I turned down into a subway, the Danube running above my head, immense and silver and yet so silent you might think there was nothing there.

Coffadwriaeth – in memory.

2000 Light-Years from Home

"What people are these, whom pain has overcome?"
He: "This is the sorrowful state of souls unsure

Whose lives earned neither honour nor bad fame.
And they are mingled with angels of that base sort,
Who, neither rebellious to God nor faithful to Him,

Chose neither side, but kept themselves apart..."

Canto 3, The Inferno of Dante: trans. Robert Pinsky

HE SAYS HE'S A CARPET FITTER. Shows me his carpet-fitter's hands: scarred by staples and fitting rods. One of those hands is on my shoulder. I take it as a gesture of friendship.

I could tell you stories.

He gets closer.

The stories I could tell.

Yeah?

He's standing, I'm sitting. I can't see what's in his other hand. In my right is a pint of Worthington creamflow, pulled deliberately creamless with the pump nozzle taken off. I'm one sip down.

I used to lie by the woods and play my pipe. And they'd come out of the trees to me. Or I'd sing to them. Always the same song, and after a while they'd start coming through the long grass. Coming to my hand.

I look up and his pupils are huge.

And the really young ones would be no bigger than this thumb here.

Yeah?

Just sitting and singing and playing my pipe.

What song did you sing?

★

In the town of Bridgend is the Nolton Street Arcade. Thirty years ago it housed a record shop, so small there was scarcely room for album displays of Hendrix, The Mothers. In summer the door was wedged open. Walking past from school I'd hear 'See Emily Play' or Jagger's implausible despair, *when you're two... when you're two thousand...* Even then it didn't work. It was phoney, trying too hard. Not like Emily, with a school badge and psychedelically-splashed art folder, who carried it all off effortlessly. Whatever it was. Sometimes she was even inside the shop, laughing, making others laugh, shock-haired Emily who seemed to have found what she was looking for.

Three decades and six months later it's 7pm and this penultimate day of the year has reached saturation point. Black rain in Bridgend. The town bubblewrapped in mist. There's no-one on the streets and for everyone in our group The Victoria is a refuge tonight. One by one we have stooped under the lintel, its declaration unread. The Vic that turns no-one away.

And this is our company. Teenaged barmaid who looks like a Kayleigh. So let's call her that. Next, a woman who could be 80 but is probably 65, crooning 'Danny Boy' to a man who's unconscious. Not asleep: unconscious. Then the usual blonde. There's always a blonde. Good legs, I guessed at once as she reeled towards the bar. Then she turned around. A face of dry-ice. The speedfreak's adamantine deathmask. Whatever's missing from it, boredom, exhaustion, betrayal are there in spades. Men, I suppose. It's men who do that to a woman's face. But it's she who hones the edge of things. Who raises the stakes. Who is both guardian and interpreter of the night's protocols. Next, there's a young couple, part of the gang in this corner. A little uneasy, they don't quite fit yet. But there's some atavistic inkling in them that makes them want to try. Not horror, not fascination, but maybe the bravado that camouflages shame. I know exactly what they feel. And last of all my friend here with his hand on my shoulder. But no. The last of all is me.

Pinsky has us down as 'neutral souls'. Which is not as bad as it might be. But look at another translation, such as Dorothy L. Sayers', and we read of those who find themselves in the 'vestibule of the futile'. Which begins to terrify. But whatever the translation, Dante has defined us. Bang to rights. Limbo, lounge or waiting-room, it's where our souls are stalled. Their flights cancelled or diverted. Because if I was translating Canto 3 I'd relocate its action to an airport warehouse on the Canadian prairie a little north of Regina. Round about Amazon, maybe. Grey snow, aluminium walls, and a million suitcases without labels. The carousels would move an inch an hour, and under its popping striplight the hangar stretch to the horizon like a field of GM canola.

Bridgend? It used to frighten me. It probably started to frighten Emily. Where did the music go? But now I love it. Of course, it didn't change at all. I did. So I've arrested that development. Now, it looks as if the Maesteg train's in because the girls are coming down Station Hill, naked bellies, big hair, half-swigged bottles of Saint Emillion in their Monsoon bags, a tattooed Silurian posse that will take no prisoners tonight. Though tonight's only the dress rehearsal. Tomorrow night's the big night.

★

'You To Me Are Everything'.
Yeah?
Yeah. They'd always come to that.

★

I was brought up with pheasants. The females neurasthenic, the cocks like pantomime dames, white scarfed, scalloped with rouge. Drag queens in the bracken. And the chicks, grown by August into red-eyed adolescents, were mad already with their bad genes. They were bred by a man called Woods. His voice pursued us trespassers under and over the Swansea-London railway line, a voice that preserved his Forest of Dean vowels, sticky as goosegrass, till he died. Woods (ah, always *Mr* Woods to me then) lived in a cottage on the Cwrt Colman estate. He hung magpies on a gibbet. Their tails might have fluttered like Emily's black stockings. When he learned he had cancer, that his body was full of dead flowers, he propped up his rifle and fired a hardnosed bullet through his skull.

One-shot Woods, says the carpet-fitter. He's talking about the man who stalked me though childhood, tracker of Cwrt-y-felin-gwcw, steps silent in yew dust, skin white as birch bark. Which astounds me. He's too young to have known Woods. Unless Woods has become a legend. My nemesis, now a myth. Because the carpet-fitter too used to be a gamekeeper. His hand still on my shoulder. And those stories he might tell are gamekeeping stories. Here they come again.

Pheasants, he says. I bred them from hatchlings. Pullets, cocks, the size of my thumb.

Yeah. You said.

And those shoots. People who never seen a pheasant before blasting off through the fields. Over the gates. Pheasants could have had horns and four legs for all they knew. Millionaires with rifles but you'd never think it from how they dressed. And what was a pheasant to them? I'd raised those pheasants. I sat in the grass and played them my pipe...

Yeah.

Don't say *yes* like that. Like it doesn't matter. This is the story I'm telling.

★

Hey Mum, I'm fifty. How'd that happen? Fifty in Bridgend. The glory of it. What did Issa write in that fiftieth birthday haiku?

From now on,
it's all clear profit,
    every sky.

And that advice for the fifty year old poet?

Writing shit about new snow
for the rich
    is not art.

Yes, Master. But mum, did you ever meet the demon? The demon of middle-aged self-pity. Somebody wrote that when they reach fifty, a woman feels disappointment and a man desperation. And that it's rarely the other way round. You'd know. Funny, but I keep catching sight of that demon in the corner of my eye. At the X2 stand in Bridgend bus station he stepped off with the rest of the crowd from central casting. Then he was with me at the new fiction shelves when I realised the librarian who had stamped my books for thirty years had been freezedried and shrinkwrapped and probably genetically modified by her own respectability. He even sat with me in the Bridgend Radio Cabs office, waiting for one of those white Mondeos that look like barracuda to slide up the street and get us out, out with the unbaptised and the virtuous pagans, out with the hoarders and the spendthrifts, out with the gluttonous and the lustful. Take me somewhere good says the poster. What about over Acheron and into the first circle of hell, driver?

And Emily. Freaked out? Unlikely. Could she too have been a neutral soul? It's hard to reconcile the sins of the futile with those albumsleeve eyes and that burning bush of hair. Impossible to consider Emily making the great refusal, and Dante leaving her behind with scum who'd never lived. But it makes you think. She's fifty now. If she taught art or English she's given it up with relief. Her kids will be grown, her husband in the tailback to Junction 34's Granada Services tuned into BBC Radio 4 for 'Moneybox Live', learning about his pension's meltdown. As if gold had become mercury. Shapeshifting money, the trickster spirit. Rat poison for the imagination. At fifty Frank Zappa, the Mothers of Invention, even Bridgend's own Groundhogs who played with Pink Floyd in the Kee Club across the road, are long gone. But maybe Emily's trying to think what she did with all those sketchbooks.

Here in the Vic, 'Danny Boy' is still spark out. Amphetamine Annie, her eyes thyroidal, yellow as cairngorms, has put something familiar, therefore historical, on the jukebox. Maybe those legs aren't so good. Her arsebone stays undefined by rectilinear denim. The speed is eating her like a bellyworm.

Meanwhile, the couple are slowly getting into it, working out the feel of this place. I can sense their souls sniffing the air. They remind me of weasels. I was brought up with weasels. I can even tell weasels from stoats. Mr Woods let them swing between the magpies with an old foxpelt stiff as jute. Now these two weasel faces are almost smiling. Perhaps they've come home.

I glance up at the pheasant-singer. He looks as if he's about to burst into flames. And here comes the question. The question they always ask.

So where you come from? he asks. The gaze unflinching.

I take the second sip.

Next time Kayleigh better keep the nozzle on.

You can get a nice big head like that.

Here, I say.

The Daughters of Uranium

THE PRIEST LED ME TO Father Clem's room and said to make myself at home. He would be back the next day for the screening. Father Clem has travelled east to visit relatives so I take the opportunity to shower in his bathroom and use his scented soap and bury myself in the robe that hangs behind his bathroom door.

Father Clem has Full Logic and I try the CDs already installed. There's polka, as there always has been in this province, and Beethoven, the sixth symphony, the hunting horns calling to each other, the great leap into sunlight as the party comes out of the forest. Jesus, I say, I'm crying, it's making me cry, and I take one of Father Clem's miniatures from the drawer in his desk, a twelve year Glenlivet in a tiny plastic phial, and it's like dosing myself with an eardropper, but thank you, Father Clem, dark horse.

I take in the memorabilia of your pastoral life on the walls of this room: your papal correspondence, the church interiors and exteriors. There you are, a young man who stands by a bell suspended from a crosstree, the prairie stretching behind you. And thanks again for the use of this room, a room fussy in a way only a single man could make it fussy. But thank you anyway for these moments in which I prepare myself.

Because I need time, Father Clem. First stop on the tour and the film is ready to roll. I set the video cartridge myself and ran it up to the moment the titles start. I've put the *maqams* in the tape machine, three long pieces that we won't need to play through, but at least they'll give us an atmosphere of Baghdad. Ysuf Omar will chant the poetry of the *qasidas*, and the instruments form a thicket behind, the *djoze*, the *santir*, yes the *maqams* will writhe for us, we will allow their eroticism a minute or two before the film crashes into the darkness of the church, my thirty minute movie, the lights out and the audience on stickbacked chairs clutching diet sodas and Ritz.

But soon the priest will come back and say time's up. I'll have to show him I'm prepared. Though to tell the truth, Father Clem, I'm feeling a little out of it. Well, wouldn't you? Two nights ago, sitting over the 747's wing I saw explosions like two silver balls, soundless efflorescences. They were there and then they weren't. But I knew we were hit and down we came drifting out of that electrical storm onto the Jersey flats. By afternoon everything seemed to be resolved and at midnight I had stepped off the last aeroplane I'm going to take for some considerable time and was waiting at the mouth of the carousel for my bags.

But Father Clem, when I walked outside the terminal it was minus 10C. and all I owned in the world were the clothes I stood up in. Those clothes I've put on after using your shower. And the cartridge of the film, the size of your prayerbook here. So bear with me a little if I take another pearl of that sweet sipping maple whisky, or a finger of Jacky Dee. And as I know you won't mind, I'll open your blinds to the view and find in this basement we're level with the lawn and the frost is looking in through the double glazing with barbarian eyes.

Still, it's a dry October in Saskatchewan. On the sky are feathers of the northern lights, while to the west the city's neon grid is starting to glow. This part of the prairie is sectioned for mall development, with coyotes yipping behind the builders' tapes. And Clem, it seems you have it buttoned down pretty tight. Here's a full Reader's Digest 'How in the World', a Camcorder Enercell weightier than a testament, your collection of funeral liturgies. Everything a man might need. Okay, Clem, cheap shot. But you know what I mean.

Because you're getting a good deal. I'm showing the film, so bringing people into church, all faiths and none, young people, the politically radical. For what that's worth. And you're giving me a room and three meals. Which is fine, I've no complaints there. I share the food of the oblates in the refectory, filling my glass at the blue bulb of Culligan water, ladling myself farmer's porridge, macaroni soup. All those men have retired, those men who married Christ, staring out at the prairie that now will not thaw for five months. I listened to them talk. Their languages are Romanian, German dialect, big frosty consonants that fifty years in this country couldn't soften. There was a nurse applying eyedrops to a priest too old to read. I saw the rheum in his eyes like strata'd snow, the strata that will soon build against the residence walls, its yellow, its violet piled against the basement glass like marrowflesh.

Did I say these men had married Christ? Clem, you all married the winter. And it has widowed you. Who was with us in that kitchen but the ghosts of children not conceived? Or wives not taken? The blind father crooned a lullaby his parents must have sung to him, parents born on a different continent and in a different millennium. There was a football game on TV and one of the other oblates was describing the plays for that purblind saint. Notre Dame huddled and ran, huddled and ran, their helmets shuttling moons, and the old men thumped chair-arms or laughed into their knitting.

Clem, last night I lay under your duvet, the one you have decorated with photographs of the Virgin, with photographs of yourself before the church that stands white as a saltblock on the prairie, the summoning bell on its scaffold. And I dreamed of the daughters of uranium, their hair afloat and their bones ablaze. They drove the Culligan water pickup truck around these lawns, dropping the blue vessels off the back while we gave chase.

But we never caught up, Clem, although we've been chasing them so long. The daughters sang with the choirs and the congregations and the sweetgrass elders as our movie lit the dark, sang the hymns that you have taught to generations. Then they ran barefoot into town, breaking into malls and gymnasiums, the daughters of uranium, Clem, stepping out of their farthingales of fire.

I saw Americium beside the river. She was rollerskating down Spadina Avenue in her iceskater's skinsuit, the little black box on her hip playing the songs of the mad composer. And Thorium, I saw her walk into the lobby of the Bessborough Hotel. What gold she wore, its wires at her wrist and ankle, a crucifix on her throat inlaid with Zuni turquoise, and so much baggage, the porters straining with the padlocked chests. You think her grand, Father Clem? Then you can't have seen Plutonium arrive from the north in her Cadillac Fleetwood, her chauffeur a great chief of the woodland Cree, and the Prime Minister whispering into her ear behind bulletproof glass. Because these are our daughters, Father. You have daughters too.

I watched Berkelium on the college stage. Remember her? How

beautifully she danced for me, taking off the mortar board and graduation gown, breasts goosepimpling in that ultraviolet pool, her belly speckled like a pickerill. She curled up on my lap and whispered the song that was meant only for us. That's you and me, Father. You and me.

You think I'm inventing this? That it's a fantasy? You need to understand all of it, as I am trying to do, as Monsieur Becquerel tried to understand, the dread and then the excitement gripping him as he opened his desk in the Paris laboratory on the first day back from the holidays. One hundred years ago, Father. Or was it yesterday?

Monsieur Becquerel looked in his desk and the black stone he had locked up was still there. But something had come out of the stone. Its soul had appeared, a stone-shaped soul that sat glowing by its side like a negative of that stone. That was the pandemonium stone, Father. You'd think he would have shut that drawer for ever, knowing what we know about that stone. But he was like everyone else. He was enchanted. We're all enchanted, Father, and now it's too late to change. Call them angels. Call them criminals. Rub their telephone numbers off restroom walls, but our daughters are out there, running a tab.

Now, Clem, I hope you won't mind if I borrow your toothpaste. Arm & Hammer, spearmint fresh. There's plenty here. And a comb would be useful too, and a towel from your cupboard, and maybe a couple of those miniatures from the collection, and a saltine or two from the plastic box. And I'll take a bar of that soap and this pair of blue socks. Red you'd miss, but no-one would care about blue. Or black. So I'll take a black pair also. And a pen from the desk and a writing pad, you have so many, so many letters to write, the papacy even, and you with no family in this world.

As I said, I'm bereft. The lightning magicked my luggage away. I sit in your room tonight with nothing to my name but the clothes I arrived in and a roll of film already set up in the church. Tomorrow I'll walk around Sears and remake myself. I'll stand as a new man in the department store mirror, every stitch on me brand new, every dream a brand new dream, River Island and Calvin Klein crawling on my skin. Or should I wear the sky as a shirt? Pull the tamarack around me as a winter coat? To tell the truth, Father, I think I was struck by that ball lightning. It rolled down the wing and into my head. I keep thinking about what happened. How there was an explosion. And then another. I waited for a third but didn't see it. And no-one else knows what I know because they were asleep, three hundred people in masks and earplugs, trusting to the air.

Then we floated down. And there was America, all spits and nesses, its summerhouses hidden in the dunes, a city like a spilled toybox. By the time we touched the runway I was transformed. So maybe I'm an American now. Maybe to be an American you have to be hit by lightning. But whatever I am I'm different from what I was. I see new things. I see that wolverine in the bathroom, Father. Once it would have frightened me. But once I would not have seen it anyway. There's wildness around us everywhere we go. I understand that now, like the hunters coming out of the forest. Below them are the vineyards and fields of wheat, around them lie the shadows of the trees and the forest smell they will never throw off. The symphony is over and there are no more tears. So perhaps I'm not as out of it as I thought. Perhaps this is what it's like to be different. To be a man struck by lightning and alive to tell the tale.

I brush my teeth and comb my hair. The priest is here, waiting at the door. He says the audience is ready and my host eager to begin. But what a pity you'll not see the film, Father, or sit with the others in the darkness as the credits roll and the music starts. Already Yusuf Omar is chanting the first *qasida*. Yusuf's voice is green as the Euphrates and as sweet as dates. It is filling the basement and now this room, the old men listening to a voice that has come back to us from Babel and which flows out of the church and over the whole city, a green voice to irrigate the parched places that are everywhere we look.

Father, you know what I think? I think I should be up and dancing to such music, as the tabla starts and the eerie santir, dancing with Monsieur Becquerel who holds the soul of a stone in his hand, as the strings of the *ud* announce themselves, dancing with the nurses and the fathers with their blind eyes. Yes, that's what I should be doing. Dancing with my daughters in these travel-stained clothes.

In the Fever Ward

THERE ARE PEOPLE WHO NEVER know where they are. And they don't care. Take this place. I came off the motorway, down the sliproad to the roundabout, took second left and drove into the carpark which was already so full I had to find a place in the overspill. I walked through the cars to the entrance and pulled a trolley out of the back of the line.

So here I am. Sainsbury's, the biggest Sainsbury's for a long drive, an out-of-town, redbrick Sainsbury's. Yet how can I be sure? It looks like Sainsbury's, for here I am, at the doors that open automatically and here I am, inside, and to my right within one metre, a display of special offer sandwiches-to-go upon a chilly pilaster.

But in the carpark I noticed traces of what this place used to be. The trees give it away, the pines they didn't cut down, and which remain, incongruous here in out-of-town shopping land. But it's not the pines I'm talking about. It's the wall. There's not much left now, a few metres of grey stone at the far end of the overspill, so normally there's nobody to notice. But I noticed the wall today and remembered it. I used to look at that wall every day and dream what lay beyond. Today it's the motorway's eight lanes and central reservation and slip roads and roundabout system but when I was here before there was nothing like that. Only the moor. The moor was red at dawn and red at dusk. At other times it was grey or green, depending on the weather. The moor changed as the sky changed, I noticed that, the cottongrass blowing like a parade of white flags, a flock of birds arriving, departing, a smudge on the sky, plovers I would have said then, a flock of lapwings that were themselves the colour of the moor, moving as if a piece of that green and acid earth could be flung into the air.

There is avocado in those sandwiches. There is brie and blackberry and rocket and salsa and honey-cured ham and parsley in those sandwiches. Those sandwiches are special offers and they pursue me into the first aisle, the vegetable aisle. But I am not interested in sandwiches today. I am not hungry today, which is some kind of victory in a place like this. A place like Sainsbury's. No appetite, or at least an appetite under control. Or an appetite for things not to be discovered in a Sainsbury's sandwich. Which is some kind of victory. Because today we're all appetite. We're mouths that walk. We're tongues that wrap themselves around the world. We want to taste. We want to suck. Christ, it's an oral world out there and everybody is just sucking it up.

Spoiled for choice? Not when you can have it all. Except me, that is. Me with no appetite today and no promise of it returning. Here are sweet potatoes in a plastic tray. Starfruit like secondhand sex-aids. Yams that once you see them in all their yamishness are lumpenly proletarian and not exotic at all. Because here's *Yam*, one of my favourite words, on the label before me and the yam itself disappointing every expectation. A failure of yammery so to speak, for these yams do not live up to my sense of possibilities. These yams have denied my imagination.

So, no, none of these. Not one of these in my trolley today. That sanctum is reserved for other fruits. Christ, I'm only up to broccoli and have a vision in my head of a man, an ordinary man in a plexiglass cabinet, well chilled, starving himself to death. A warning to people like me, as he becomes thinner and thinner and still refuses to participate in the feast. Because that's what it all is today. The supermarket is a temple and shopping a feast. In which we end up eating ourselves. So there in his cabinet he refuses sandwiches and starfruit and chooses endless aceticism. And we push past with our trolleys, with our breadfruit and our sweet potatoes and give him not a thought. A starving man in his supermarket tomb? A man who diminishes but never vanishes, a man like that hunter they found in the Alps, exposed in the ice, sneezed out of the glacier's running nose. With his quiver and pointed shoes he seemed a fashionable hunter, a leather pouch with his private things, and over all, his skin brown as a yam. Yes, a man like that in a supermarket chest freezer. You'd think, it must be a special offer. Like the sandwiches-to-go.

The grey wall must have been circular but that's the only section remaining as far as I can tell. I used to look out of the window at that wall and no wall, I was convinced, could ever have been higher, no wall could ever have been built that kept people so effectively from where they wanted to be. The Great Wall of China was a kerbstone in comparison. The Berlin Wall I might skip across. But everywhere I looked there was a grey wall on the horizon. And even that was behind glass. Because there was a glass wall too and behind that was the rest of the world and in front of the glass I lay on my stomach in striped pyjamas and a man told me to take off the pyjama trousers and then he slowly pushed a needle into the roots of me, a needle which he held there for forty years, needling into the bone, into a place that was inside my bones. I know it was forty years because every year he asked me to count, and I began and reached forty and the needle was still inside me. Then I counted again and slowly it was withdrawn, so slowly, it took age upon age, and when at last the hypodermic was free I saw it was filled with gold.

What that man took from me I didn't know but after he had gone I lay in my bed and looked through the glass wall. I lay in a yellow room, I remember that, a yellow room with three beds, mine in the middle. I stroked my arms, felt the knuckles of my spine where the needle had entered. And I feel a little like that today. No appetite, a bit unsteady. I'm at the first terminus now where I can turn right into the next aisle, which is tinned goods, or linger here at the dairy section, a bright pasture indeed. Perhaps it has something to do with last night.

Because the story of last night my sister told me this morning. There she was at 1am in the passenger seat of a car coming east on the motorway. Driving the car is a colleague and in the back seats two other colleagues. They're all tired, and except the driver, everyone's been drinking. It's misty, but visibility isn't bad in the dark, though the motorway lights are switched off. Well, maybe visibility was bad if the lights were switched off. I know that road at night. It's a dark corridor from childhood. And down that corridor they came, maybe doing sixty, ready for the slip road, then fifty, and there he was. The ghost. The ghost of the boy. Or the boy who looked like a ghost, a blond ghost who peered for a nanosecond over the bonnet of the Volvo and into the windscreen where my sister and the driver looked back, a pale boy of sixteen crossing the motorway at 1am.

They hit him like a Kango hammer. Out of his eyes fled his

ghost, the ghost of a boy of sixteen, and the windscreen exploded as his face was pressed against it, pressed between the darkness and the glass, no primrose pressed more palely within its book. The windscreen shattered and the glass cut all my sister's exposed skin. Every speck of it. Her friend the driver stood sobbing on the hard shoulder while the two friends from the back seats found the boy who had been hurled a long way and rested him beneath a barrier. The car was crooked as a butcher's hook, the Volvo's steel plates rent and buckled by the bones of a boy of sixteen. One of the friends telephoned the police. Soon the blue light of their car was livid as a Sainsbury's insectocutor.

Crossing a motorway is no fun. I'd rather cross a river than the motorway that runs outside this supermarket. I'd rather cross the Ogmore which races behind the hill or the treacherous black Danube through Budapest or the Rio Grande that the wetbacks swim every night of the year. But whatever, the boy was dead. Which as far as I'm concerned is appropriate. Because many people have died here. Died on the sliproad and died on the roundabout and been found dead in the overspill. They've also died, I reckon, in tinned goods, where I stand now. Beans with bacon and beans with sausage. Own label beans with no frills. Old El Paso refried beans in their yellow tins in a trial offer pyramid. Yes, people have died where I stand right now in the second aisle with an Old El Paso tin in my hand. But no, not refried beans today. And maybe not any day if I continue to feel like this.

Because these were the fever wards where people of this county were brought in their delirium. This was where one day I was carried in the back of a car, wrapped and delivered like a rose with a long stem, a boy in a blanket delivered to the isolation hospital that stood on the moor behind the wall. Here, I remember child after child arriving. I could see them through the glass, all wrapped like roses in white laundry, their heads nodding against the shoulders of the men who carried them, children like roses, feverish and white, held in towels as if their skin was too hot to touch, as if they were fragile as porcelain and would crack and break apart if they were not wrapped again and again in the ward's white sheets.

They lay me on a bed with a bed on either side. Or that's what I've been told because I was deep down in my dream world. They carried me from the car and into the isolation hospital behind its glass wall. That day I had walked in a wood called Coed yr Hela, the wood of hunting, the wood of gathering. I had seen animals in the wood that normally I never saw. But that day the animals were present, talking in their own languages which I found I could understand.

In the bed on my right a boy sat crocheting. I had never seen anyone do that and I watched him from the corner of my eye, afraid to ask a question. But soon he turned to me and showed me the animals he was making in red wool. And yes, I had seen those animals before. I had seen them in the wood as the fever arrived, the fever that brought me to this room. Coming from the wood I felt my body grow stiff. A headache assumed its own identity within me but soon I lay within the headache, imprisoned in it, strapped down in its white chamber on a white bed, scaled like a lizard with the fever's steely sweat. There were metal rods in my limbs. I could not move my head; a metal rod had been forced into my backbone, all the way down that hollow trunk. I dreamed I lay with my bones exposed, I could feel my bones stripped of their flesh, I lay like scaffolding in that room the headache made for me.

The boy looked up from his needles. He smiled and held up the first animal. It was an owl. I had seen that owl in the wood, a little buddha on the bough. He held up the second animal. It was a snake. I had seen that snake, a viper, in the wood, a black viper with hollow teeth, pilot lights burning in its eyes. It was coiled under a bush looking at me. But I had never seen anyone crocheting before and did not know what to say. The boy smiled again and nodded his head and continued with his work.

In the other bed there was another boy. He lay whimpering under the sheets. That made me feel good. It made me feel brave to think that someone else was crying in this place, terrified in the yellow room. I wanted the boy to cry louder. I wanted to see his tears and to feel his fear but he lay under the sheets and whimpered and I could see only the top of his head and his blond hair, the blondest hair I had ever seen. And then I went back to sleep. A nurse brought a supper tray but I did not look at it. Sleep was the meal I wanted, and the drink. I dreamed that night of a banquet of sleep, a white plate of white soup, its white meats fragrant and dissolving in my mouth, a white cake decorated with white pearls such as women wore, but these pearls I picked one by one from the cake and felt them turn to liquid in my mouth, pearls on the cake and candles too, white candles burning with white flames that no matter how hard I tried I could not blow out. I had no breath. I was all bone and lay as a skeleton must lie, a negative of myself all through that airless night.

Lime pickle? I'll give you lime pickle. That stuff can do damage to an unsuspecting digestion. And here's a bottle of paprika powder. How I love to sprinkle paprika, its red speckling like a trout's belly, love to throw it into the air and see where it lands. But no, not today. Still nothing in my basket and I am in the fourth aisle, the aisle that Marco Polo must have built on his way home from the spice lands. Because look at this. A bottle of chilis, labelled very hot. Each chili has a face pushed up against the bottleglass. Some might call them malevolent, these expressions, filled with malicious intent. But not me. I hold the bottle to the light and see reflected at me the faces of the children who once lay in this aisle, tossing on their beds, throwing off the blankets in their fever, the children who dragged dreams out of their heads before they died in those beds, before the dreams became too powerful and the fever burned them up like fireworks. Because this is where they died. In the fourth aisle of the supermarket. Right here where the packets of poppadums and naan bread fill the bottom shelf and jars of fruits line the top. The children in the yellow room died of fever. For every death there was an inquest but no-one held an autopsy on their dreams. No-one asked me about the dreams we shared, no-one asked about the animals we had seen, the animals I saw in the wood. Because doctors never ask questions like that. They merely wrote down that the children had died of fever. But listen to me. I was there. That fever was shared between us. It held us tight together in our fever-tribe. I know why those children died. The children in the yellow room.

So where was my bed? Sixth aisle maybe. In the middle. Between the boy with his parcel of red wool and the boy who cried. The second night I lay half awake. The man had come again in the evening and opened my pyjamas and put the hypodermic into the dint of my back. Again it went beyond my bones into some unnameable place. It didn't work last time, he said. We have to do it again. So once more I counted, one to forty and waited, and in my head went backwards from forty to twenty-nine, to nineteen, to… After ages, the needle had made the return journey through the corridor in my spine. And I looked around again as it came free and saw that the hypodermic was filled with gold.

I was half awake. He was shaking me. I felt his hand shaking me, the blond boy, the boy who cried. And in the darkness of the room we rose together and went through the glass door in the glass wall and down the passage and out through the entrance hall. Far away we heard voices. They came from a room with a light that shone through a spy-hole. But soon we were outside with the dew soaking our pyjama legs, the blond boy leading and I following as if I was still dreaming. There was a full moon above with a ring around it and it was easy to find our bearings. We walked over a lawn to the pine trees. These were blue in the moonlight and their branches spread like reefs into the sky. Beyond the pines we reached the wall. The blond boy was already climbing, telling me what he could see from the top, his head straining to look at the moor as it did to peep at the room from beneath his sheets.

The next thing I remember we were in bed. The night nurses had followed us to the wall and taken us back. In the morning I lay and watched the first boy knitting with red wool, knitting an animal that had no animal shape but would soon, I knew, be one of the animals I had seen in the wood. The blond boy lay hidden under his sheets. I could hear him crying but when I spoke he did not reply.

But, I told myself, we had been to the wall. Surely it was not a dream. Yet nothing was different and no-one spoke about what we had done. If it was a dream it would be the best dream I had dreamed in that place, that room full of dreams. Because the dreams were stopping now. As the steel rods came out of my body so the dreams began to fade. I could raise my arms, place my chin on my chest. Today a nurse had given me a lesson in walking. Because, I knew, I couldn't walk. So if I couldn't walk, I wondered, how had I reached the wall? The nurse wore a white pinafore and when I fell I felt its roughness on my cheek. She picked me up and the glass of her watch was cold against my skin. I fell again and she held my face in her apron. Tomorrow you'll be fine, she had said. Tomorrow will be fine.

The seventh aisle is the most colourful in the supermarket. It contains boxes and bottles filled with cleaning fluids. And so many of them. But then, there is so much to clean in this world. Baths and lavatories, floors made of linoleum and floors of stone. And all the glass in the world, like the glass wall that ran around the yellow room. And then, all these clothes we wear. Because our clothes need cleaning too, and our bodies and our hair and the insides of our bodies. We have to rub and scour and rinse. How I love those words, those cleaning words. How clean they already seem, rubbed and scoured and rinsed in our mouths. So here I am, in the seventh aisle, and only the eighth remaining with its frozen foods and then the vineyard of the wines. Which is good because I'm tired now, tired by walking up and down the supermarket. As I said, I'm not at my best today. It seems as if I've been walking here for days.

Which, I know now, is a miracle. The nurse had said tomorrow will be fine and she was right. I tripped and staggered and she made me get up, again and again holding on to her hands, feeling her uniform against my cheek. And yes, by the end of the day I was walking, surely the first in that ward to walk again, the first to leave the dreams behind. And how wonderful walking is today between the polishes and toilet ducks when I realise that this is where I learned to walk. Learned in the yellow room to put one foot before another and walk as I had done in a previous life, the yellow room that no-one believes could have existed in this place, to walk as I had once walked in the wood, and seen the animals and heard their secret speech.

That night I was tired and slept without a break. When I woke there was confusion. Loud men moved behind the glass and there were police officers scattered across the moor beyond the wall. On my right the boy sat knitting with his red wool. On my left was an empty bed. In the night my friend had stolen out again and this time had climbed the wall. The nurses were crying, his parents were there beyond the glass, holding each other as if they were only now learning to walk again.

There's a long queue at the checkout. Sainsbury's is full today and all the tills are working but there's going to be a delay. And also, there's a strange atmosphere. People are talking in the queue. Whispering. Maybe I should start listening instead of comparing what we have in our trolleys. From the cleaning materials in aisle seven I went down frozen foods pretty quickly and avoided alcohol altogether. Usually I like it in that boozy nook but not today. So I wait in line with my trolley and think about the woman ahead with her Häagen-Dazs and her superscoops and supersizes. When I think about it, I'm not a bad person to stand next to in a queue like this. You see, I know where I am. I know what we are. I understand miracles and I am a connoisseur of dreams. Every day is our last day. Death awaits us like the lover we thought we'd never find, that one who always looked the other way. And then she turns her thrilling gaze...

Don't step away. Please hear me out. No matter how many air miles Sainsbury's are offering, or loyalty points, we're all going to the same place. Because I know where I am. You think I'm making this up? Look outside at the pines with their black branches. Look at the grey wall in the overspill. And something's coming up the line. Like mist, the mist of rumour, turning to gossip, to the dirty, disappointing truth, something's coming. When she sees the mist one of the checkout girls is led from her till. She is crying. The people in the queue should look angry but nobody complains. They should look worse than if someone was paying by cheque for five items or less or offering a fistful of special offer coupons to a staff trainee. They should be looking daggers at that girl but there's no anger here today. Something must be up.

Apparently he worked here. In this supermarket. The boy who became a ghost before my sister's eyes, the boy who peered into the Volvo before it hurled him into the fast lane. He worked here collecting the trolleys. Pushing wagontrains of trolleys from the overspill back to the trolleypark. Stacking shelves in the dairy department. Sixteen years old they say he was, and out celebrating, his head full of something somebody had given him. Out of his head apparently. So far out. He was trying to get home but the motorway lay before him like a river. He had walked out of town past the supermarket, silent at 1am and come to the motorway. I can hear it now, the motorway. Behind the grey wall it runs where the moor once lay, as far as anyone could see. I used to look at the moor, red in the morning and red at night, the plovers in a swarm coming down to land. Now the motorway runs there as wide as the Danube, as the Rio Grande. Down the slip road and straight across the car park he walked, where the lawns used to be, black with dew. Then he came to the wall and climbed over. I used to think that wall was the greatest wall there was. Then one night I learned different.

There's another girl come off checkout now, being led away crying. Normally customers would be angry, but today it's okay. You see, the problem is, some people don't know where they are. And some don't want to know. And standing here, waiting with everybody else, I suppose you're wondering what's in my trolley, especially now that I've told you what the woman ahead has bought. The man behind, by the way, has seventeen plastic flagons of cider, seventeen microwave pizzas and seven sacks of ovenchips. Soulfood.

How does that make me feel? All I've got, to even the score, is the usual. I've got what I've always got, nothing more or less. And yes, it is a shame, I can understand people being shocked. But that's because they think they're in the supermarket. They think this is Sainsbury's. But I know it's really the yellow room. To me, it will always be that room. You see, I learned a lot in that room. Walking was not the half of it, my arms around the nurse's waist, my eyes wet in her groin. So you can listen all you like to them gossiping down the line. But what's important here is a sense of history. Because as far as history goes, I think it would be better if you started listening to me.

Josephine's Rain

The Fair

I threw a dart and it won me my wife.
I fired a rifle and the prizes were my children.
I put a coin in the slot and lost everything.

At night my caravan rocks on its bricks. By morning the sand has
built a reef around the door. In the darkness I hear its grains on the
glass. That's a language I am learning. Brother, sister, do you hear
me, I am learning the vocabulary of sand, repeating it in the nights
when there's not a sound but sand explaining how one day all this
will be its empire, and how sand will have taken back everything
we have won from it. And I believe it's true.

I bet on the white car and it came in first.
I bet on the black car and it came in first.
I bet on the red car and now there is only sand in my pockets.

Evenings I'm in the arcades. Penny-falls, video-poker. I'm there
with a gang who always turn up at the same time. We hardly speak
but someone said that down the coast you can play all night and
keep on playing through the morning and there's never need to
stop. But this Funland is all rules. I said to the man in the booth, I
said, mister, I got nothing left. I bet the smoke in my mouth. I bet
the holes in my belt. Very good holes those were too. So I want to
bet myself, I said. I want to wager myself, mister. Do you know
what I mean? I asked him.
   My self.

Go home, he said. We're closing now. He didn't understand how
serious I am. I'm nothing in this world if not serious. So I watch
the wheel where my children sit in the sky and the carousel where
my wife rides her painted horse. I bet on the red and off they went.
Any other day the red would have won. Now how faint those
voices are above the fair.

At night in the caravan I lie on the floor. The sand lies on the floor beside me. It strokes my hair. I lie on the caravan floor naked because today I lost my clothes on the Colossus. And the sand whispers to me.

I love you, says the sand.

Do you understand? it says.

Even the sea is silent.

I love you, says the sand.

Would you like me to tell you a story?

And the sand keeps whispering. It puts its tongue into my ear.

Did you ever hear, asks the sand, did you ever hear how much gold there is in a mouthful of seawater?

Glan Ogwy

I LOOKED FOR SHALLOWS but there were none. First step would be man-deep, straight off the wharf and into the current, the current more nimble than one of the kids in this lot riding on silver scooters, the lot full of rattling weeds, the kids far out on the current of language that was taking them away from me, and the river itself tight as a dockyard hawser, a fleece of wires green and inseparable, the wires of water running in its joy.

Although the river was fast and the boards were broken in the wharf, this was a safe place. Because not everywhere was safe. I had stepped out of the train on North Six or West Seven, I don't know, I was tired and confused, and there I was in a current of language. A current I couldn't recognise. Yet I felt it as it tugged at my sleeve, then took me by the thighs as a current takes you, sweeping everything along.

Motherfucker, said the radio voice in the shop doorway. The current was in my mouth now. Motherfucker it said again, or perhaps it was the hooded child who said it, who held the radio in the shop doorway, big black box of a radio. But I was up past North Seven or West Eight, looking for the street whose name I knew. But there was nowhere to cross the river, there was no shallow place in all that place of language, and there I was looking down on the roofs of water as they collapsed, on the floes of foam, on the dead dogs and the plastic that writhed in the current in effigies of men, at the barges that passed on that current, loaded with the city's waste, the city's sweet and smoking rubbish going to the tropical islands we gave dollars to for taking our secrets away, our sweet and smoking language, such a succulent tumour on the world's skin.

But this was safer than the other places. There were no hooded children here, no black boxes with their words spat out so hot I could feel them burn the sidewalk behind me. Who was I fella? Who was I mister? Well, I thought, I'll tell you who if it comes to it.

But I was gone, gone past that storefront with its black box of language, the impossible words all hung on their hooks in the darkness of the shop, every word on its hook, a butcher's shop of language, blood on the floor and blood of words on the hands of the hooded child, raw words under the glass counter, words pierced with wires, the eyes of words empty and the mouths of words blackened and agape.

I never liked children, you see. I always understood what children are capable of. Even these other children on their silver scooters. So I walked on, oh brother I kept moving over the hot sidewalk. Away from their demonry. From their outlaw music. Away from their heraldry on the walls. So here I am. By the river. Out on the wharf where the barges once tied up to iron cleats and the bargees threw their lariats, whooping at the land. Now I am out on the wharf looking into the river that offers no crossing place. Because there is no crossing this river, no fording it at all.

Instead, you step in and feel the water slide over your head. And once you're in you're in and there's no coming up. Once you're in. Which I learned the hard way. Getting off the train on West Seven or North Six and meeting the demon in his robes, listening to what the black box said. Yes, I learned that all right. So in I go. Straight off the wharf. You ready to come with me? You ready to step straight in with me, to let go and sink into the current that rushes past, full of honey and blood and the pleading arms of men? Listen. The river is speaking. It's time to go, motherfucker, says the river. Time to go.

Josephine's Rain

After a while they nod and give me the key. So at 8pm I climb the steps and unlock the door and here I am. In the lighthouse. There is no daylight now and the sky has collapsed but here are the keepers' coffee cups fathom-lined with use, and here are the charts that I know so well, their geometry of the coast. If I look perhaps I'll see stars between the clouds that should start flying soon, coming in from the west with cargoes of rain. Josephine's rain I call it because the storm is called Josephine and everything about this storm blown to me across the ocean is Josephine.

I stood out on the beach this evening and caught the first drops. They felt like a gift. A blessing I should call them because a blessing is a reward and tonight the storm rewards me with Josephine's rain. The tower taps the sea with its blind man's stick. So many nights I've walked the avenues waiting for her. Down the prom and through the fairground waiting for my lover. Because that's what she is and she knows it herself as those others never knew it, how could they understand me, walking behind them as I did, their bodies like blue pilot flames flickering over the esplanade, so delicate you might hold them in your hand and watch them play over your skin. And as I'd walk I would look into the windows of the hotels or down the corridors of the Kingdom of Evil. Sometimes I've followed them inside. Don't they know, those others, that the ocean is impatient for their company? Come with me, I've whispered against the glass, or as I sat watching at the bar, sipping my seawater.

But I can forget them now. Tonight Josephine arrives out of the west. There is rain against the glass, Josephine's rain, and the waves have already reached this tower's base, waves with no colour in them – unless it is the beam itself making its circuit, or the Hi-Tide when its door opens and light escapes from its spirit bottles open mouthed and forever pouring. But there is no-one out on a night like this. Even the SkyMaster is locked up. The fools are frightened of the immensities. Every storm is a reward but so few are worthy.

There are nights I've stood on this promontory and the waves have travelled over my head and not a drop of water touched me. I've seen the sea's architecture, arches and aisles where the congregations are prostrated because above them are angels or the electricity of angels countless in their consortia. A miracle some would say but the storm protects its own. And now it's all around me and I feel the tower sway with Josephine's rain against the glass and even the beam itself is extinguished as the hurricane daughter climbs the stairs I climbed when the town was still awake and now Josephine is at the door in her wedding dress and oh at last my handsome bride.

The Kite

THE WIND SLAMMED A DOOR. I heard it, running upstairs. There's a storm coming, mother, I said, but mother was gone out to the shore, picking up shells like little death's heads, a pelt of sleet on her back.

Storm coming, I called, but she was way out on the sands now, and those sands blowing east to west, horizontal drifts in the stormlight, rattling against my legs as I ran after her, the seeds of the storm in a horizontal hail, the sand fleeing from something behind the headland, something terrifying there, even the sand running away from the storm, and there was mother running on the beach, a silver coat of foil her armour against the storm, a silver suit the nurses had given her to protect her from the cold, to keep the heat within, the blood heat, and she lifted her arms like a silver bird and the gale took her, I saw it stoop down and her arms were wings and she was up then down again, then up again into the air, a kite shrieking, its silver arms outstretched and the shells falling from her hands, those handfuls of barbiturates dying like smoke signals on the air, up and up a hundred feet, above the sea now, the sea that was tearing itself apart, and the horizon mauve as a vein in her arm and she was gone, a silver dart, a gull off the promontory, yes, she was gone but in this stormweather that blows so hard I know we will follow soon enough.

Because the thunder is speaking. As lightning bursts upon the rock. As lightning lays its hand upon the sky. While in our house the doors are locked and the wind paces its feverish room.

Gwter y Cŵn

THE SEA TURNS BACK. But it won't go far. Yet this afternoon its retreat is like no other. Usually the waves here are polytunnels, shredding themselves in the wind. But now the tide is crushed and voiceless. Or perhaps that convalescent murmur, that is the sea.

This is the one hour of the year I can move around the promontory, down the old red sandstone bulwark to the limestone karst, that landsker where geology's language changes, down to the crevices and gwlis and overhung beaches that are usually no-gos, exclusive as some Mediterranean enclave, whitewalled, camera-scanned. But rarer, these. And never named.

It's also the hottest hour of the year. The first beach is no bigger than a bedsheet. But such linen. And rich, I find as I get down on hands and knees, rich in swart rubies, big as Californian strawberries, and turquoises set in silver such as the Navaho wear, who had heard rumour only of the ocean. There must be a fortune here.

But my own beach will be the next beach. The sea, introspective, is one yard away, yet shrunken into itself, as far removed as I will ever know. This sand should not be touched. Hard to imagine when the last footfall was made but I step in and leave my mark. Here is red wrack like cassette tape. Here are the mouths of anemones in the sand, as if the shipwrecked lay under these few grains, hearts still beating. And there again, that convalescent murmur. A little louder now. And now here are stars of the sea in purple and gold, dead it would seem, a colony wiped out, but I know these dead can breathe, that they wave, imperceptibly, to the sun and the tide and at the turning of the world.

Behind the beach is a cave. At the entrance there's a sandal, right foot, Woolworths brand, disposable and disposed of. A yard in is a plimsoll, left foot. The isopods race around like armoured cars.

From the cave-roof descends a lead weight with four wire barbels, attached to a plastic line. It hangs like a bellpull. I pull and the silence rings.

What now? I stoop in. On the cave floor is a shirt or some other garment, wet, it will never dry out, a sodden red and black tartan over-shirt, winter-wear or some grungy uniform ripped off. Again, that murmur, a little louder now. But in I go, further in. Here's an Adidas sports bag, still zipped, dented one side, bulging the other, one handle broken. The sand is dark here; there is coal dust in it and snailshells green as gulleggs. The cave is bigger than it looked, the entrance a-dazzle with southern light but farther away than I would have thought. Almost a tunnel mouth. Now this is a pair of sunglasses, scratched and salty. After a while there's a place in the cave that is room-sized. On a shelf are a bottle of Dr Pepper and the plastic wings that held a Somerfield tuna mayonnaise sandwich.

I stop. Here is a doll with no arms and no head. Just three black holes like the nozzles of the anemones. I need to think. Here limestone meets sandstone. Border territory, never named. Now here is a child's windmill with blue and yellow corkscrew vanes where no wind ever blew. On the sand lies a photograph album, its pages covered in polyurethene. I open it with my foot. Blurred images, indecipherable writing. But there's the murmuring again, the beating of the starfish hearts as they point to where the sun goes down and the tide turns. Suddenly I am looking at a photograph of a man barelegged, barechested, the beachcomber type, hands on hips in front of a cave. Around my foot the sea has slipped its first white vine.

Rhych

ONCE I STOOD NEXT TO the Yorkshire Ripper in the queue for candyfloss. I saw Osama bin Laden licking a ninety-nine. Good times. But those days are gone.

Now up my sleeve I've taped the microphone wire, its little black nose against my wrist. And the sea leaps into it, the voices of those I never meet preserved forever. But this is as far as I go. Every evening I come here and understand the limits. This far, no further. Tonight the sky should have a high pressure swell moved in from the west; there's a new moon visible between clouds. And ahead are the gatekeepers with their new moon earrings and their samsungs, the uniform of the elite, gossiping to each other one hundred yards apart while scanning the faces that come through the gate under the barbed wire and into the arcades. Into the Camp.

I've tried being different people but the gatekeepers see through every transformation. A child with an inhaler, a woman with a diamond in her navel like the eye of a wolverine. I could be all of those people. I could be a black chick in Rayban's, a white man in barrowboy Armani. I could be a plover, a palomino, a viper with a voice like chiffon, a sandhopper out of the dunes, small enough to hide behind a raindrop. But no go. They see me every time. And back I come to this peninsula, allowed to watch but not to join, as the sky grows darker and the wheels glow brighter in The Camp.

Now the BeachParty is opening and closing and the people within it first laughing then gasping their fear as the speed increases. I can hear it opening, closing, all its tiers like the blades of an army knife, open, closed, open, red now, red now violet, violet now red, open. As it comes to rest people reel out of their seats and try to brush the light spores off their skins. But it's a part of them that will always be there. They are X-rays now. It's got inside.

Because I know what's going on. I could warn them but the gatekeepers know that I know. They look for me on their patrols. In the Camp office the commandant gazes down through perspex that changes colour as the rides go round. I've seen inside that office, the screens of the computers, the mountainous download. Facts, figures, evidence. It's all there. I've tried hacking in, sent viruses superbly wrapped. But no luck. Because there's no-one else who understands what's really happening. In the boxcar that climbs between gulch and cactus; in the mirrors of the tattoo studio; in the ghost train faces that come alive when the siren sounds – there's no-one there who understands.

Now the crowds pour through the gate in the wire and the gate-keepers whisper into their mobiles and the lights flash in the arcades and the money rustles like the tide behind me. Everyone is expectant. Even the commandant in the tower staring down on the crowd's heads. Those isopods on a rock. In his hand the commandant holds a file, a mass of papers with my photograph scanned in.

The thickest file of all. Yet the crowd never looks up so never sees him or understands. It never asks why or how. But keeps going into the karaoke bar, everyone a celebrity, on to the SkyMaster that sends them skyhigh, or to the Beachparty that shakes them as the sea would shake them, their skin tingling as with a new tattoo.

Tonight it's bigger than ever. And much louder. The Camp's gone crazy with that end of season desperation when everyone is afraid they might miss something and this is their last chance to find it. Fools. I could fly above them but they'd shoot me down. I could tunnel under but they'd drag me round by the heels like Hector in the Trojan dust. So at home I play the tapes. I put the cartridges into the machine and sit in the darkness. The sea plays over and over. The sea never stops and the tape ends. Then I play the Camp. I listen to the rides and the machines, the people coming in, what they take away and what they leave behind. All night. All night my tapes in their black boxes. Better than Schumann on the brink. Better than *Mystery Train*. All night until tomorrow when I come back to Rhych and its sea-ploughed rock. A man refreshed and ready to be admitted. To be allowed. Ready once more to tell the truth.

The Wilderness Lake

I THINK OF A LABORATORY at night with one gas-tap left on and the cold the colour of the invisible gas and its smell the smell of the unsmellable gas that fills the room. I think of a brazier within my chest at which flames lick and curl. I think of a hood pulled over my eyes and my body crackling in a suit of cellophane.

And now I am so cold that the cold has its own identity. It talks to me, crooning and nuzzling, taking me onward by the hand over the ice, a pleasant fellow the cold, a companion on the lake who knows the way forward and knows the way back, which is good because I am lost on this continent, in its very heart I am no-one, but the cold helps out, my twin today, of my height if a little more slimly built, the cold my guide and confidant, strange how quickly he has learned so much about me, my middle name for instance and the credit card expiry date lodged next to my heart.

Ah, Cold, I say. Now not so fast. Tell me about yourself. Show me photographs of your children. But Cold only smiles and talks about the eagles he saw once flying south in the shape of a base-ball diamond, and how sorry they made him feel because it was his company they were escaping, as if bald eagles were afraid of something as ordinary as cold. And then he talks about how diesel freezes and how men must climb from their cabins and warm the pipes, cajole them to liquidity, how once he laughed at a man skewered to the earth by his own urine frozen straightaway as he pissed a yellow arc like the bough of McDonald's in the blazing air.

Listen, Cold, I say, I've heard that tale. It's a legend in these parts that everyone believes but is not true. The next thing you'll say is how you once saw a child on the highway frozen to a stalagmite. How it stood at the roadside for two weeks before drivers realised it was a boy turned entirely to ice.

It's true, says Cold. There was a tribe lived on this lake that used to worship cold. Their weapons were made of ice. They shot wolves with icicles. The cold was a god once and will be so again.

But then Cold holds up his hands and says, you're right. These are fables. They make the journey pass.

And in my turn I tell Cold about another place where water never freezes like this water and where snow like this snow never forms a reef, grey as hoover dust, pitted by snow-lice, but where cold is a man who paces his room with a symphony in his head but all the scoring wrong, and where cold is a woman who covers a floor with nails, recycled nails all black with age pulled shrieking from their first snug homes. And where the man and woman live the sea is colder than this, the sky is colder than this, cold sand, cold stone, ventricles of foam bursting under the feet of anyone who ventures out.

For a while we are silent and walk on across the lake. There is no horizon because the sky is also made of ice. And one thing I can say for Cold is he never complains. But he is brooding, I know, so it's not unexpected when he whispers, 'stop'.

So we stop and Cold points in a direction that might be north or south because I have no mind now for the right path. Over there, says Cold, a long way off is the shore where the tamarack grow. Under their branches is a cabin and once in summer I looked inside.

Maybe we should start walking again, but Cold has gripped my arm and he is heavier than I thought. He stands there in his logo'd skater's suit that says Marlboro and CBC. In his glittering fleece.

And when I looked, says Cold, I saw a man like you. Outside the sun was terrible, one hundred degrees the thermometer said, with blackfly angry on the lake and a wasps' nest like a hockey gauntlet hung in the porch. On his bed the man lay still. I held his hand and it was blue to the elbow and colder than the diesel pipe. Colder than your symphony. I felt his feet and they were cold and blue to the femur, both feet cold as hockey pucks.

Cold stops.

You ever play hockey?

I shake my head and Cold continues. In his bed on a summer's day the man was turning blue. But I could only watch his eyes, big and white as the blue advanced, those blue crystals filling him up. His eyes were white and mad. His body was vanishing, shutting down, the pistons stopping and the oil all draining back into the sump.

Now Cold holds me tighter by the wrist, so tight I'm sure my hand is turning blue.

He froze, hisses Cold. To splinters. Here on this lake. Froze on a summer's day.

Then Cold smiles.

Walk on, he says, and points the way. Before you catch your death.

The Irongate

NEVER TURN YOUR BACK on the ocean. That's the best advice I ever gave, but there she goes, the child in her espadrilles, her steps making no sound but her soles of quicksilver and the shadows of her heels so swift to erase them, the child who carries the star she has found, a creature out of the storybooks, one that confers power on its discoverer. There she goes towards the esp but what am I doing but ignoring my own advice on this day of the lowest tide, with men picking out soft-bodied crabs from previously inaccessible inlets, anglers further out than they have ever stood, casting for bass or for the simple fact of standing on these unknown sands and watching their lines fly further south than they have ever flown, children wading round the point that is only now exposed, and myself even further out, the current around my feet, the water of no colour six inches down but green and chill a little deeper, infused I tell myself with some quality of the deep, the deeper sea out there, the inestimable deep, where the bass are mirror-fleshed untouchables that have never towed a line and the sun's light is fierce on these waters and behind my eyes, even though my back is turned to the horizon now and I am moving away, the only one but for the child who goes in this direction, the child who is carrying her prize away from the ritual, and the eyes of the crowd upon me, the man who walks out of the waves, out of the forests and wrecks and hissing playa of the new land, the land we had never known before today, a world the tide has disinherited for these minutes only, until it too turns and comes seeking.

Never turn your back on the ocean. Behind, I hear it filling my steps as the child's steps are already filled and there is the mouth of the Irongate into which she peers, into which she steps against all protestations, the weedgreen Irongate darker than a lugworm's burrow, the tunnelmouth of the Irongate that leads out of the waves and into the town's crypt, a place that is seen only on days of the lowest tides, our eyelet in the ocean, reinforced concrete annulus hooped with iron and its backbone of brick, our fathers' engineering that they hid from us in the ocean and which has revealed itself today, with the sky like a library, burning, aisle after aisle of pages silvering, and a squadron of sea-magpies touching the waves and the child disappearing into that doorway, stooping her head and stepping inside, and the bathers shouting and a windsurfer hung from his parasol shouting, and the bodyboarders shouting and the crabbers prising their faces out of the pools and shouting, and sunbathers shouting though they see the world in negative, and the fishermen turning away from the water at the very moment the tide finishes its retreat, that moment when time freezes and the blood comprehends because the blood too is salt, and then the child is squeezing through the grille hung from the tunnelroof, through the Irongate itself, and for another moment that grille is a grid that divides her body as if apportioned in some diagram, every limb and organ glossed, numbered for some purpose, and we see the stars of her flesh in a momentary constellation and then she vanishes from light as her footsteps have already vanished, those steps like thistledown that every astonished citizen has watched blown across the beach.

Gwter Hopsog

I CROSS A DESERT and at the petrol-stop a man rises from the bed he had rolled out on the rock and comes towards me. We stand together, wraiths under the wire of the moon, and he offers water, the smoke of cigarettes. There are soldiers here who stare at us, boys in grey uniforms without dinars for water or smokes, who have dug themselves in against the coming day. Along the perimeter the plastic bags tear and scream, plastic sheets that must have wrapped something enormous. Hail falls out of the dawn sky and disappears and the wind mooches around with nowhere to go. Nothing has grown in this place for millennia, the earth has blown away and all that is left is a man in the desert whom I have wakened and who stands with me in the greyness of the world.

But I think of the sun and I remember another life, my obedience to light, carrying out its commands, prostrating myself on the rock shelves, in the hammocks of the waves. That simple life. I closed my eyes to the blood-coloured world and dreamed as if it would never end. But greyness returned. Really, it was always there, but secretive, biding its time. Now here it is, a world of razor wire, a world of abrasion, the salt gilled like refrigerator ice, a grey liverwort around each tarn. Feel how it seeps back into the picture, out of the limestone, blood out of a stone, grey blood flowing out of these lagoons and around the megaliths, the waves become finials of ash and somehow in my hands there are grey chrysanthemums that I have taken from the shrines built where the sailors died, as if time was playing backwards now.

Yet I have learned to love the grey. In the desert the man looks up at the Mesopotamian stars and shivers and draws his coverlet close. The soldiers sit on their heels in a circle and the plastic shrieks on the wire as the wind races past, coming from nowhere, going nowhere, maddened by the nowhere that has overtaken us all. Yet in this other desert, many things grow, for every limestone seraglio is presided over by creatures without brains and without hearts, laser-guided, instinctive killers. And around them are their enslaved populations of rock-borers, sand-sifters. These hermaphrodites live without families, without birth. Their histories have been devoted to the weapons they use, the wrecking ball, the nerve gas. And then to the speed with which they can kill.

I look closer into the grey. Gradually its evolution is revealed – the ossified lilac, the fossilbeds of gold. And there is nothing else to do but wear this grey, to pull it around my shoulders like the *jalabiyah* and wait at the desert pools where even the rocks have sprouted teeth and struggle, stone against stone, to the death.

Pwll Dafan

THE OCEAN? I'M AN ADDICT. Littoral-minded to a fault. Each day it's like opening a sack of nachos and rustling about until every sharp corner is gone, every crumb of sodium rousted out and devoured, my mouth sore, my fingertips tingling. So here I stand again at the inlet's edge, the tide retreating, the strips of weed green and steaming as the sun comes on strong, the iron showing through the concrete, Mexican red like my Astra, the barnacles in their nursery, blowing bubbles like babymouths. An ocean addict all right, drawn once more to the cadenzas of the waves, all their varieties of venom.

Over on the rocks where the waves break like flowers of the Russian vine, there's a bass fisherman casting into the melee of cream and grey. Bass is a big noise now, swish fish, swanky restaurant food, served with a salt crust. So what tastes, I ask, but the salt? Seasalt coarsely crystalline, as here on the sea's rimrock in the evaporated pools are rings of salt as if tiny fires were lit last night and all that's left are circles of ash. And the rock itself is the colour of eclipse light and those birds of the eclipse, the rock pipits, the same colour. Strange how they sang all through the occlusion, their two notes okaying as the sky turned the colour of limestone and the people down here passed round welder's goggles and the little circles of salt shone momentarily brighter and the limestone-coloured birds called in lust or alarm or for the joy of it, while in Pakistan seventeen people killed themselves because they'd thought the sun, reduced to a cuticle, Mexican red, was being swallowed by a snake in the limestone light.

But think of that bass laid out white and grey like the pages of a book. The diners carefully lifting the words, devouring some, leaving others, too easy, too foreign, trying the lemon or the samphire that garland each page, and coming back always to the salt taste, which is the taste of blood, our own taste, a familiar secret we carry wherever and however.

So I scrape the moss of salt, a dirty miniver, out of the rock and take my fix. That nacho taste, fierce, of something that's doing me harm, and the sea's full of that taste, the sea packed with preservatives, of E122, of E160c, of sodium benzoate, 100% RDA, full of unimaginable salt. Think of the Dead Sea. A blue inflatable armchair. And here, every wave a salt-quarry, every high-pressured lacklustre swell a sump of salt and sharp little fragments of corn that scald the skin and excoriate the mouth.

That's what the bass fisherman's after, casting into the prows of the waves, the salt falling over him like grass pollen or a pall of nox. There's so much malevolence in the sea, this is why I've come here again, to see the mankiller heaving itself over the rocks, its power half exhausted but still worth marvelling at.

Because yards away on the promontory, white with the bonfire rings of salt, is where they laid out the drowned from the Samtampa: those salt blistered bodies, those men who had drunk the sea and died of their meal. Their banquet of salt. That's why I come here again and again, for the challenge of it, the precarious steps that only the pipit can make look easy, shimmying its tail, cocking its limestone head as if to say, follow me, it's okay, another step across the saltpans, and then another, don't worry, it hasn't even begun to be dangerous yet.

Cwm y Gaer

THERE MUST BE A SHORT-CUT, I think, a quicker way back to that room with the fan's propellers beating as quickly as I could make them and the light endlessly brightening. Here's what I've bought: biscuits and bananas and orange Fanta's icy aluminium held against bare skin. Immediately I step off the track I am petted by the rain but soon the rough treatment begins and my Dakotas are anthracite and my denim is stiffened and black. And I am only ten yards in as yet, ten yards out of the piledriving sun and into the forest that erects thorns against trespassers and hangs lianas with jellyfish stings over any bare flesh.

Everything wet here. Ladles of rain tip out of the treeferns and rain smokes out of the seed canisters on the forest floor, out of the moss's suction pads. Every tap is turned on, every jet into the sauna at full pelt, and down I go, ankle deep, knee deep in the mangroves, so deep I see at once I might never recover and so pass beyond the tutelage of botanising and turn into a tree root, a twisted black manikin of mangrove-coral, spirit of this place, legend the locals laugh about at the lanchonette.

Time to think. What's around? Seeds that germinate before my eyes, fatal fruits growing ripe and softening in seconds, falling into the mulch and rooting themselves for a one thousand-fold come-back. An orchid erupts in front of me and already it is waist-high and wide as a brazier, its helmet steely, its leaves green metal and the mottling on its leaves reputedly Christ's blood but those spots are surely the flush of its own fever. This orchid has a voice, rain's lubrication on its cogs and pulleys, and it seems closer now, so close I can feel its heat and the hydraulics of venom in its thousand mouths.

And I thought everything in this place had been discovered, so close are we to the sea, the red road dinted with tyretracks, stepping half an hour ago out of my lodgings without my shirt and walking up the track past the swamp. Its surface seemed full of bubbles until I saw that they were toad-eyes that were following me all the way to the palm-thatched *barraca* where a woman was collecting moths that had died in the night, their bodies heavy with gold dust, their wings also full of eyes, some black, some pale as that beer they drink here, ah, Antarctica, stacked in its crates, our wild toasts last night at the forest edge but so far away now, that time beyond entreaty, so far away as I writhe in the thicket with the rain scalding my chest and my feet underground and the exquisite black cilla of the orchid mouths waving as the rain passes over us.

For there are many of us I see now – those who have wandered into the trees and found no escape. Messengers with satchels held above their heads, cultural attaches with tape recorders, oil company executives whose suits are blueprinted by bougainvillea. Close by, an environmentalist stares into the screen on his nokia. No escape yet, but there is always time. Perhaps they are waiting for me to do something, me the newcomer, most recent visitant of that world beyond the trees. I peel open the Fanta and take a sip. In this sodden place where I am ever thirsty. So, I think. So, so, so. I tap the can against my teeth. Now the first thing we must do is... Don't worry, I'm thinking. Any moment now, gentlemen. Any moment now it will come to me.

Twmpath

REMEMBER, PEOPLE VANISH.

That's what the pilot says as we approach the mesa, the ground below us adobe red, and not a sign of water yet, not a river running or brief arroyo, we'd have to go as far as the Verde to see water, the Verde that never dries but rolls on under the cottonwoods, flattening itself in stillwaters where children bathe and antelopes sip from the shadows of the manzanilla.

One day here, the next, who knows. But gone. Vanished.

What shines are the tops of the automobiles we see down there, so far down the heart itself falls sheer away like the wall of the butte, the windscreens glinting and the sun catching the chromium fenders of the convertibles you still notice around the state, Chevrolet Impala say, a gliding mass of metal that tells the story of another age, stately barges those, so grand they make me think of some old pharaoh out for a Nile cruise.

And the pilot says what's strange is that we weren't looking for a lost civilisation. No sir. We were taking photographs of the mines the uranium companies dug out in the desert and even on top of the mesas, so high above the plain, the miners must have taken days to reach the rimrock, camping there above the desert floor, their night fires otherworldly and set amongst the stars like temporary constellations. Now we bank to get a closer look at this summit, kiln-baked in the noon light, the discarded gear clearly visible from here, old workings and pieces of metal hardly rusted, so dry is the air, my throat telling me it's too dry, I have to chew a mesquite twig to soothe the raw burn, and with that and the nausea from being up here in the first place, it's not the best of days. But the pilot keeps on.

All that was here, he says, was what they built out of the dirt, those lost people. Empty rooms with clay floors, hard and cool, maybe a few pots. By the time the first settlers arrived, they were gone hundreds of years. Gone before the Spanish came through with their horses and armour. The Hopi and such like, they never went near these ruins. Ghosts, you know. The desert is full of ghosts.

He banks again and my stomach lurches and I feel the warm rush from the open window and we're so close to the top of the cliff it feels like I could step down onto that summit, step up to its battlements in their black felt of shadow and emerge on the rampart, the whole rock like some sailing ship, wasn't that what the anglos called it now, a galleon of the desert where no-one but the miners had stood since the ghost people vanished into the sky. One ordinary day. Leaving their chilis drying on the ristras and melon seeds on the floors of their tenements. Stepped straight out of history as if they'd gone behind a rock for a piss. Not a trace of why or where.

But it's not that hard to imagine, if you really think about it. In fact everywhere I go there are people who just left, doors closing and conversations that died a moment previously still suspended in the room, like the antelope leaving its hush behind on the air and the air still holding the idea of the antelope or the shape the antelope made on the air.

Yeah, beautiful, man, says the pilot. Real beautiful.

And the aeroplane halts on its rail on the fairground floor.

Ffynnon Wen

HERE I AM AT THE BORDER and the man takes me across the cement into an office where the controller sits. The controller is tired. Tiredness has entered his every cell. Here he waits, and in waiting has grown old, old as a coelacanth under the pillars of the Atlantic, bottom lip wide and jutting, eyelids closed.

I place the bag on his tin-topped desk and undo its ties and pull the zip. The first man cranes over as I lift the creature out, showing its green eyes and computer heart and great shuttered indigo mouth. Out it comes into the evening light, out of its nest of weeds, its gills trembling, its antennae flat. How small it seems now, crouched there in its shell, but the first man is impressed. It is what he thought it would be, and he nods and says yes, here it is, and he is thoughtful with it, reverential. The controller looks through one cracked lid. A cigarette droops on his lip.

I am touched by their care. I have carried this creature a long way, cradling it in the bag, watching the faces and the hands of fellow travellers as we bucked across the emptiness, the driver at ease in those black lands, the shepherd boys waving, the petrol tankers roaring empty the other way, the loaded tankers behind us and ahead, for even the desert is ceaseless in its tides.

And now the sun has set and left a last angler on the precipice, line far out in the petroleum dusk. His light burns at his feet, no bigger than Venus already visible, something he has reeled in, some luminary that crouches at his side. But already he has cast again, into an evening that teems like the desert in June, its chafers burring, its moths with their golden epaulettes butting the air, gold dust heavy on the moth-horns.

Inexpertly I open the creature's eye and show how its bones interlock and how the zeros will dance along its skin once the sleeping heart is stirred. Yes, breathes the controller, and slowly he stands and takes the creature from me and holds it to his chest, stroking its shell. Yes, says this man in a stained white shirt, who decides the destinies of anyone who would pass the window of his room, that smoky aquarium: some towards the wire in the east, some towards the western wire.

And look here, I gesture, pointing to the mark on the creature's skin.

Ah, says the controller, testing the word.

A sound that emerges from the Atlantic floor.

Then, *Sony*, he says. Ah, *Sony*.

And the other man nods too, because this is a famous creature, and they stroke its shell once more before I replace it in the bag amongst the weeds.

The fisherman will cast as long as the night lasts or the sea hurls itself against the stones beneath. His star stays at his feet, quiet now as the SkyMaster that has wheeled its constellation over the town, its music finished, its silhouette still. While all the other stars shudder and dip. The fisherman waits, a watchman who will see the dawn, a guard who stands at the border on a night that is never really dark, these comings, these goings not unreckoned by him.

The SkyMaster

THEY SMILE AND ASK how I am then close the cage and drop its bolt and there are always two of them, one lean, one squat, both tattooed, lean with oily hair, squat with a bristle cut like a smudge of newsprint, lean being Johnny and squat's name a mystery but both are servants of the centrifuge who polish chrome and scrub the floors, for this is new, this launching pad, its smell is new and its colours free of the resort's oxides, those pavilion faces sunk into beards of rust.

At the beginning I envied them. What nonchalance, I thought, as they set us off. Such skill as they danced among the cars. They presided over the well of gears, cleaned up where riders had been overcome, so many are unworthy. But they'd rather spend their time laughing down there, turning chemical eyes after schoolgirls. Johnny rolls up his sleeve and shows the burns on his arm, those lovebites from a cigarette. He thinks he is a warrior but warriors do not proclaim. Sometimes they smirk at me but it doesn't matter. Hirelings of the gravity master, they will be gone with the season. Up there is another country that is waiting my return.

First. Forget the sea. The sea is barbecue ash. But the land is a fire that will never be put out. See how its flames race away, the gorse ablaze, each spindle tree a nest of coals. See the road's platinum dust igniting around the Texaco forecourt, on to the Odeon glowing like an insectocutor on the Cymdda. Such purpose. They laugh at me but only from this seat climbing towards the sky do you see the order of things, each of us in our appointed place – that field of sunflowers and every one with its face towards the south, the Tesco lorry stopping at the roundabout.

So this is how the world works. If I glanced away it would vanish. Or chaos rush like seawater into every street. I'm high now, above the arcades, beyond the Kingdom of Evil and soon there are plains and cities behind their city walls, and then armies marching, meeting, falling apart, then deserts where the lightning strides and the sun rising and the sun setting and far in the distance something I can never see because the car starts its decline so slowly you would think we were travelling on into that unseen space. I want to cry out to the gravity master in his cubicle with coffee mug and newspaper to take us higher, master, higher, put down *The Sun* and loose the chain but there are the armies again and the city towers reaching up to us burning and imploring and then the plains where lightning beckons and then the spindle trees incendiary now and here is Johnny and his stigmata, poor pierced Johnny with the buckle on his tongue, Johnny who must have seen what I have seen but never tells, Johnny who must rush to free the cars, but of course I'm the only one today because the one who rides is the one who rides and so I'll wait here for a moment, eyes tight shut.

Tusker

It started at the Texaco garage. One evening the queue was a little longer, a Capri at the front trembling with drum 'n' bass. The next morning there was a cortege of motorists backed up to the roundabout. Then bread began to vanish from the shops. I listened as the story was promoted up the news hierarchy. By 10pm the next day it had reached the pinnacle, buses without diesel, forty tonnes of Zanussi looted on the hard shoulder. When the population searched in vain for merlot and chimichanga I knew. I knew there was nowhere to go but chaos, that place we thought was locked up tight, the dark mansion hidden behind its trees that Stephen King had never glimpsed.

How easily the crowds swarmed in. They were the ordinary ones, neighbours and friends, all desperate to save themselves, with the loaves breaking and spilling from their hands, a Sainsbury's mango rolling down the street. Prophesies fulfilled themselves, events siring events. And beneath the anger, beneath the fear that came out of nowhere and the strange new odour, rockpool-sweet, of freezer-juice, the power gone off as the grid ran dry, beneath the hubbub of the new regimes, I heard an exhalation of relief.

Where there were lights on shore are black gantries. Sailors escaped from the harbour and now there's a scuppered hire-boat blocking the approach. Smoke rises, stops, and rises again from different summits in the dunes, and in the bonfire light, shadows loom over the beach. There are people who tried to reach this place but their leader drank seawater and went insane. I heard him on The Irongate, keening for the technologies that melted away like a wafer in the mouth. Others will follow and already the dunes are full of failed prophets, but few can stomach salt, the sea's manna, which was always the harvest of this peninsula. Salt and sand, the twin gospels. Men will look hard to find redemption here.

Their time ended as I knew it would. Think about down the

coast, locals carving their names into that beached whale's velvet hull. Eleven tonnes, never seen before, the leviathan's gift of himself. But nobody understands omens now. Maybe I could teach them how to live in these new times but I'll stay silent for a while. Let it calm down. For as always the waves race to my feet and bring me what I need. In the afternoon when there's no shade, I listen to the catechism of driftwood. And count my rewards. For what am I but a driftwoodsman, a rockpool reflection crowned with sea-holly, who has mastered for himself the dangerous trades?

The tide has come in and covered a world. The old ways are irretrievable yet life goes on. There is no mourning, only the dancers in the bonfire light with voices of celebration. 'Free', they shout. 'Free, free.' Or maybe I'm wrong. At least about that. Maybe somewhere in the darkness there's a bird singing. A bird I've never heard before.

★ ★ ★

A Glossary of Soup

IT'S LUCKY I'VE GOT THE STAFF. Well, the boy who comes in today, that simple sod. When I take them on they can't even hold a knife. But they learn. There he is now, cracking a marrowbone. Needs strength, but this recipe demands hot syrup. And there's nothing like marrow in soup, its yellow ore.

The broth is simmering. Three minutes to go, I calculate, holding back the rosemary. Three minutes for the leaves to soften, their power to... diffuse. Difficult herb, rosemary, that crafty aromatic. Some say it's a better perfume than a food, but I say different. Here I go, counting the nails from my rosemary bush, greener than gorse. Yes, rosemary, I say. My old lover. We know each other so well.

Some of the others call me a mercenary. But they're just as bad. The truth is we go where we're paid to go. These days people give good money for what I can offer. It's a skill. No. A talent. But it's more than that. It's a lifetime commitment. It's everything I've learned and also it's wherever I've learned it, because every place is unique.

I look out the kitchen window. How wet Wales is. Or maybe England. The border twists so much here no walker can tell what country he's pissing in. There are castles small as dunghills where only nettles grow, and country inns where the country food is straight from the chicken tikka factory in Hounslow. But not here. Everything in my kitchen is made in my kitchen. Outside on the blackboard they're chalking the day's specials and in the car park the big series BMWs have already arrived. There's a jazz singer in, and a comedian. A gentleman who writes for *The Sunday Times*. Three months here and I'm famous. Or at least, my soup is famous. Soup, you see, it's always the soup: cavefood, babyfood. So I make them pay. For the talent. Which is the essential ingredient. For the education. Because as I say, every kitchen is different.

Here I'm out early mornings when it's misty and only the crows are up, grumbling in the dew. I follow the hedgerows, the medieval ones with their hazel and stagheaded oaks. A few weeks ago they were overpowering with garlic leaves, but I use the flowers too, a white garnish with cheese, and sorrel, delicate with the glans of a woodland mushroom, and the sage flower's almost-indigo, and hawthorn leaves new and pale, and the tiny yellow cogs of nettle-flowers, and the nettleleaves too, the greenest green in that hedge world, and those grapes I can never resist, fat and red on the bryony vines, those too, what a sauce they make, and the sly night-shade, looking at me with its tipsy eyes, who could resist such succulents? It's all I've learned, you see. It's education. And they're paying out fortunes, the newspapers, the TV, the owner of this thatched shithole the luvvies wet their knickers about. They're paying for soup.

Yes, soup. It's serving me well. I remember the soup I invented at the Fuschl Castle in Salzburg. Such a kitchen. Generations of imperial filth had left a golden patina on wall and ceiling. The last skiers would come down about four. The previous night I would have had one of the boys trimming the garlic, three hundred cloves every day, stripping the haulms and cutting off the cuticles, all that paper at his feet like a child on Christmas morning.

Soup, soup, the skiers would roar, and there would lie the new peeled cloves, white and curled under my steel, and soon I would add the onions as out there in the firelight the skiers would demand my soup, my creation, and I would look into the dining room at the girls taking off their caps and unlocking an avalanche of hair and the young men with dark curls and perfect skin. That's how you tell breeding. By the skin. Soup, they'd shout, those aristocrats, those laughing Hapsburgs, their genealogies more intricate than frost, banging their spoons on the board and raising their purple kir, and there I would stand in the kitchen, bringing their soup to the boil, the cream gone in, the wine gone in, adding the parsley and the nutmeg like a benediction, the drops of spunk from my warm cock as I knew they'd desire it, desire my soup in its frothing pan and the boy pouring it into the tureens and the waiters carrying it out to applause, my soup that would now anoint their chins, garlic soup that would chase a glow into their eyes, and tonight their love-making would smell of my soup, their cries to each other in an ecstasy of soup, cries and supplications as the logs burned down and the snow crept through the darkness hiding their trails on the glacier and the smoke from my kitchen rose in a single spire.

But winter was chilly. I had to leave. That was my wandering phase, though to tell the truth, I don't stay anywhere long. I hate routine, or routine hates me. I'm an inventor, but try patenting a recipe. Anyway, food's my passport. It takes me everywhere. Once I drove into a town south side of the Black Mesa. Got a job washing dishes at the Sundial Motel but soon proved I was better than any staff they'd ever had or are likely to have again.

Mexican soup, the señor said.

What about it? I asked.

Can you make it? he said.

Does the moon shine? I asked. Is it hot as hell outside just now, most likely up to one hundred and ten, do coyotes bark in the night? Of course I can make it, I said.

Good, he said. Get into town, we need those peppers pronto.

Three weeks later every miner for fifty miles was parking his Ranchero outside the motel. Every rodeo widow in three counties was driving her girlfriends up to the Sundial and I can assure you not bothering to consult the menu at all. Mexican soup was what they wanted and Mexican soup was what those hungry boys and girls were assured supping.

I put on gloves, a mask and sunglasses and then I'd commence cutting the *habañeros*, little polyps of gunpowder, or like something you'd find in a rock pool. Such diabolic fruits. Day by day that soup got hotter, son-of-a-bitch soup I called it, and of course the customers started challenging each other. Who could take the strongest soup? Who was the biggest sumvabitch in the Sundial Motel? There were groups that ran books on it, there were champions proclaimed and champions deposed, great chili kings who ran weeping out the Sundial door, dogged trenchermen who stuck to the task even though their eyes were streaming and their lips blistering and their bellies must have been vats of molten stone. Like they'd spent all day breathing chipotle smoke. Before they gave up. Pushed away their plates and stuck their head in a carafe. Except the one. Peabody they called him. Shy Peabody from the uranium mine.

So the señor is selling beer by the pickup load as well as the soup. And fair play, I'm learning too. Because a talent like mine is always restless. It can't stay the same or it becomes no talent at all. I was working with limes which I never really thought about before, and dark little *tomatillos*, and an Indian boy would peel the *ajo* and his sister crack the *nogales* out in the courtyard by the sundial itself, crack them with a pebble out of the Verde river.

That soup meant everything to me. Every day it was different, lemons and limes and pumpkins pieces, goatmeat, rattlesnakemeat, such a delicacy in those parts, I'd make a real *menudo* they called it, the halves of the walnuts that the little girl would bring from the courtyard gathered in her dress, acorns like the Apache used, beans and nixtamal, all the Mexican parsley I could get in town or at Wal Mart. The tomatoes and squash I planted myself, swelling on their umbilicals. But chilis were the thing. Chilis like you've never seen, Big Jims and anchos, the *serranos* that were hot enough for almost everyone, and those *habañeros* grown by the devil himself. Gila monsters the cowboys called them, those big oafs fanning themselves with their baseball caps.

And for Peabody, who would always come back for more, folding his workmates' money into the backpocket of his jeans, there were the pepper seeds and a pinch or two of that special ingredient from up off the mesa behind the town. Yellowcake, the Navaho called it, a few grains from the rock that the miners left around. Don't ask me what it tasted like. Even when we were lining up the tequilas after the Sundial had closed I wasn't stupid enough to put it into my mouth. It must have tasted like the desert, I suppose, the desert where Peabody had always dug. Sumvabitch, he'd say, smiling his shy smile, the uranium tailings grey on his boots, and I'd smile back, telling him oh boy Peabody, you've done it again, you've beaten the cook of the Sundial Motel. Then Peabody would raise the spoon to his lips and his cheeks glow with pride.

The writer from *The Sunday Times* is not interested in our blackboard. He says he wants me to create something unique. Especially for him. Which, of course, I was always planning to do. My privilege, sir. Outside the rain falls on the border. A Mercedes gleams like caramel. Sometimes I long for the cold again and see the glacier that groaned by my kitchen door as I leaned against its ribs with a cigarette. Or the irrefutable sun as I poured dishwater on the tomato vines and sat chopping the *cilantro*. Perhaps it's time I was off once again. Planning things for those who live to eat. Because this is how it always starts, a listlessness, then a hunger to be away. I lift the lid on the pan. Ah, nicely. My kitchen's aromatherapy. We're almost there, Mr Writer Man. And I throw in the rosemary, just a few green nails.

Nico

WATCH HER A MOMENT and be aware that others are watching you watching her. Blonde, with a crimson streak; small face under the blusher. Listen to this creature as she takes the stage in the Four Sevens, one look at the karaoke autocue and then she's off, eyes to the ceiling through this asphaltic air. Nico she calls herself, clinging to her thistle as the wind shaves the cottongrass. Too much mascara maybe but the mirror in the Ladies will be the judge of that. But love, heartbreak, the big rhetorical chords? She knows every verse, there's not a chorus she hasn't memorised. There she is, as the thistledown flies round the carpark behind the sports centre, word perfect in somebody else's song. She has spent her life in this place, singing her heart out. There could be nobody better to guide us through.

Because it's a curious place. Some never know when it finishes. Others cannot say where it begins. But all would agree on one thing; they know it when they are there. So this might be a beginning. Yet who would come who could not go elsewhere? And who would stay who wasn't held by loyalty's ligature? Either way it's a straight flight north towards a range of mountains. Out of the carboniferous goes the road, over the limestone that surrounds the coalfield and vanishes towards those anvil-headed peaks.

There's snow on the highest, a tonsuring under the sky, whilst beneath the ridge on our left is a lake. Today men fish its waters, acid as they are, but once a hoard was lifted from the bed, a shield, a helmet, chariot gear, all gifts for the journeying chieftain embarked upon his metamorphosis. As we descend there is one larch left on the hill. It hangs like a fox pelt above the splintered wood. The other trunks have been hauled off. Coming past us up the gradient is Johnny Owen, hooded and anointed in his own perspiration. As he passes he swings a right, a left, changes a tape in his walkman. Nico waves but Johnny is uncertain of how to address the female of the species. She sings him a song:

Never been kissed, Johnny.
Never been kissed.
Will you ever know
What it was you've missed?

But he's looking sharp to me. Almost ready for the world title. Now here is a colliery. Men in orange step frowning into the light. This is where they understand borders and border-crossing protocols. There are many borders in this part of the world. Down the dip is where the Aber boys rule, their leader with the cloven nose, zinc-grey strides. He stands bristling on the first inch of his territory, he who was once an auroch, a nightingale, and is now a guard dog in Factory Terrace. Over at Asda, Gwydion is buying texmex and World of Soap; at Jack Brown's there are those who watch the screens whose mothers were necromancers. They look away, tearing up the slips. Impossible today, impossible tomorrow, but the day after tomorrow, there will be transformation. And no matter how hard the Aber boy strains, he cannot reach us. There he bridles, girning on his leash. As we cross into his country he's left biting at the air.

No-one sees us at the Flats where people speak a different language and trade in outlandish currencies: blotting paper, silver foil, the pollen that smokes from the cups of a capsule. Nico has seen all this before. She's still whispering her song:

We'll lay you down, Johnny,
We'll lay you down
In a silver blanket
On the golden ground.

It's a song I try to learn during our zigzag flight to the Royal Hotel. This is where Taliesin rents a room and his cylinders are delivered every week. Today as every day he sits in the bar sipping from a glass that never loses its head. In his book of tides he writes of the everyday things. This is the fate of Taliesin. To write the list that will never end. And looking over his shoulder we see that today he has added to it:

the breasts of Lara Croft, like the shoulders of a goshawk, hunched and bronze. How the boys with Algonquin quiffs,

learned in numerology, proclaim her divinity, she who has
already withered to a stick:
a Brick Row mastiff in chevroned harness and belly-belt;
the Darren's dreadlocks after two weeks of rain, every waterfall
on its bwlwarcau squeezing from a tube of smoke;
the signal mast on the Werfa like a hatstand of sombreros;
Oxford Street air fired with fenugreek;
the infant on the memorial bench, in one hand her nokia, in the
other her inhaler;
the mastiff's keeper who has adopted the dog's gait:
the Chinese dragon of blackthorn all the way from Cwm Gelli
Wern to Cwm Nant Hir.

Down below there are flags and cheering. No-one notices as we
slip into the Lucky House. We can watch the match while waiting
for sweet and sour ribs, although we already know the result. But
everyone in the crowd knows the result, no matter how they shout
and yearn. In their bodypaint, their sacrificial clothes they understand it is only safe to shout when it doesn't make a difference.
Making a difference is dangerous work. But here come the ribs,
pungent in their pyx, and soon our mouths and fingers are crimson with their delicious dye.

There are plenty of people in Commercial Street yet no-one sees
us part the thorns around Tabor and fly in. Tabor's floor is an
ossuary for ospreys. Someone has burned a CD collection and it
has melted like Dali's clock. Richard Burton will read the lesson
here next week, in a voice of phosphorus. The harmonium stops are
little knobkerries that spell *flute* and *piccolo*, so Nico plays the first
bars of *Daeth yr awr*, of *Delilah*. Nobody sings because nobody
knows the words and she gives up. The congregation kneels where
it always kneeled, but eyes closed, hands over its ears, while the
instruction manuals have been bleached of every verse. Bruce Willis
came here once, hiding out from the hitmen, his white vestment
with the words 'valley boy' a scoop of silver in the dark. Now the
daylight wheedles in through a broken slate. That's our escape
route, and Nico takes my hand and out we squeeze, past a trophy
factory with boulders blocking the car park. Nico used to work here,
making prizes. When everyone had received their prize the place
was closed down. Then at the Heads, she points to where they tried
to bury the coal glacier. Its veins still burst from under the earth,

children's faces frozen there, and behind them parrots and treeferns and the stone eyes of a hippopotamus. Down Roman Road comes Ed Thomas in a 1974 Chevrolet Impala. There's an Odeon where his House of America stood, serving test tubes of ultra-violet light.

I'm still trying to remember the song, but from Fairy Glen to Mr Patel's minimarket everything goes well. The river rolls at our feet, a chain-harrow throwing up dandelion-and-burdock bottles and coal-not-dole badges. Both Nico and I love rivers: the Fawr, the Fach, the Great Swallower of Unconsidered Trifles, the Little Swallower of Unconsidered Trifles. Nico says their waters are preserved underground in enormous museums. Rivers are prehistoric meltwater, and in darkness our perfumes eke into them as the dyer's hand cools itself at the paper mill. Here's the Fawr in spate, shimmying like a samba dancer. If we tracked it to its lair, if we became ants or aphids or used our mayfly hour for such exploration we would see a tunnel-mouth, hardly an eyelet in the earth. And beneath would be the Fawr, fossil-cold, twisting through corridors before rising up to a single point of light, white as a dipper's breast.

Now we fly down a side street and upstairs to The Beast Within. Here is Raphael in his taboo studio, his scriptorium, inking the little blue wren that runs under a sleeve. On the wall are the symbols that covered the chieftain in the lake. Raphael says he is the artist who painted the young Nico. I look more closely at her. She might be older than I thought. At last I am ready to choose my tattoo, my explanatory text, but Nico is saying it's time to leave.

As we fly Nico and I agree on one thing. If we could turn anger into ideas there would be no stopping us.

We need an anger ioniser, she says. There's so much anger in the men we meet. All the negative energy men who want to be hard men. There's anger in the air. Anger in Lewistown eyes, Pricetown mouths, the Friday night forcefield, Monday morning gravitational prolapse around Evanstown.

They should make a map, says Nico, a map of anger's isotherms. Then we could see the country that anger has created. We would see the head-weather.

But anger's not evil. Anger can be the start of things. Civilisations have begun with anger, that steroid of the heart.

Mr Evans, Mr Price, says Nico, you have overdosed on a dangerous protein. Strip off that leather coat, Mr Lewis, that has wrapped itself around you. Anger is an eclipsing sun above Taff Street, a python swallowing its tail in Ffaldau Square. Back off Mr Evans, before that mirror in the toilets of the Four Sevens. Strike it now and you destroy yourself. There you fall, all the little pieces of you, like shattered glass to the shithouse floor. You'll never be put together again, Mr Evans, no matter how hard they look for your slivers on the cement. The quarrel's with yourself, Mr Lewis. Back off. Your hour will come. Soon your children will be tall as sunflowers. Grapes will grow over the walls of Gwendoline Street. You will have learned the symbols of your own domain. So grow vegetables, Mr Price. Discover the wisdom of soup. Spread the sports section over the kitchen table and file the nipples of your Ford Orion's sparkplugs to an implacable and righteous bronze.

Back on Commercial Street, Taliesin has been out for a consti-tutional. Who else could have written

the immortal hour

in black felt on the pillar of Quids In? It must have taken a fair time, such a neat script, and Tal with the vibration white finger. Maybe like us he studied the forgotten sign for the New Theatre and went in over its reef of lights to play one of the machines. We cannot see him there, but every place is taken. We look at the play-ers at the controls, childlike in their concentration.

Never so beautiful, says Nico, as their scores spin round.

As their seconds hurtle backwards to zero.

But all is well. Nico knows the way south and out. As promised, she understands where everything finishes and starts again, and how to speak to the border patrols. Nobody looks at our papers. Even the Ton boys wave us through, expressionless, into their wild territory. And now we are in a high place on a narrow road. Far away we glimpse an ocean, while on the next hillside eleven giants are turning somersaults. Gently, we alight.

Goodbye, she says. I'll see you again if you like. One of these days.

Wait, I call. That song you were singing. How does it end?

Nico laughs. Then I realise she has always been laughing. She flies into the air and turns north, mascara blacker than ever.

End? she calls. There are no endings.

But for the last time I hear her voice:

You're the history, Johnny,
You're the history
Of who we never were
And what we'll never be.

And the gold on her wings is an arrow vanishing over the horizon,
and my goldfinch is gone like a courtesan gossiping to bed.

Mr Ogmore's Last Words

ba
baah
babah
bab ili
balal
babble
bibble
babel.
That's it.
Babel.
Babel and back.
Every day we walk in and out of its gate.

Thank you, Mr Buddle. Our bombsites will never be the same.
And I'll have another piece of Battenburg. Church window cake
we used to call it. And a glass of Barbera. For the barbarians
amongst us. And one for Barabbas of course.

What I was I am. But what I am now I never was before.

In the wood I saw ten thousand, ten thousand with their heads
bowed, their eyes closed, their swords sticky with nectar. An army
we all thought was destroyed, and in a willow wood too, a wood
without a name and not on any map. I found myself within its
room which was hung with green tapestries, and tore out handfuls
to clothe myself.

There I heard it. The dirge of the dew. And saw the archangel
bent over in his dirty mac, while the water lay in wait. What did we
call the water? The fierce stream. Ffornwg to me, its furnace at my
fingertips. Sometimes I scooped it to my mouth, all cowshittiness
and lightning's bacteria. But no matter the taste. It was mothering
milk to me. I was ready to believe.

Maybe life was elsewhere, its wars and festivals. But I was the
man in the wood and if the Ffornwg flowed through one ear and

out the other I knew what the water wanted and that under its flat stones were my own tournaments of terrifying purpose.

But what were the tapestries on the trees?

Why were such cushions placed over the earth?

That is moss, said my mind.

But what is moss? I asked.

No answer came.

Because moss must. How it must. Its moisture makes a monsoon over rocks and tree trunks, moraines of it where horizons of ancient rains are folded like table napkins, a maze over glacial scratchings, moss that cradles oceans in its nets, in its midnights when eels ford its fathoms and each moth smuggles moonlight in and out on its milky fuselage.

Then the moss breathed.

I could hear it.

How it breathed.

On my knees upon an Alhambran mosaic I listened to its tiny hubbub and heard the murmuring in its mosque.

So I became the initiate. Into my skin the moss had spoken and there was my breath misting its mirrors. Now I was the man with his mouth against the mortice of the moss.

He was fifty years further down the root than me, so a creature of the carboniferous. A grandfather and a guardian. Not far from here like some magician's trick he would disappear into the earth through its gate of language. So who would have thought that under the buttery grass of Heol Laethog a tribunal of trilobites would be debating the new Europe and Nye's dole of daylight for the soul.

The grapes grew fat in the glasshouses. He picked one and peeled it, looking at its mirrors trembling. That fruit reflecting into eternity was a-wobble in his mouth. How young its yolk but the acids in it an old answer.

Sometimes he understood. What could be simpler?

Thinning the seedlings, raking the soil, to thrive the soul needs a south-facing wall. And that is where I have tried to live. Against the south-facing wall.

Perhaps it occurred that he who had been a miner was now a minister. Surely the grapejuice on his chin was Christ's kiss. But sometimes under the panes the heat would leave him faint and he would stagger like a vine with its cruck kicked away.

But soon revived. He sipped a flinty glass and liked to leave a leek bolt and swell into a minaret. What he made of himself he made. And the night before the auction, locking the pavilion which he would never unlock again, he kicked one of his useless oranges down the greenhouse gutter. Its gleam was the only light there was, but enough to see

the chauffeur salute for the last time:

the gamekeeper hang himself from his gibbet:

the chamber maid who bobbed like a candleflame start a Coronation Street scrapbook:

the chef marry the tax collector:

the madonna with linnets:

the zebra-hide shields, the Nantgarw plates:

the Faenza bowls, the tiger with feet like bunches of marigolds, the books, the Bordeaux, the air the laughter the air, all fall all fail, the gods, the godsends, the Novello with his nougaty notes the *Rhapsody in Blue,* in blood in bloom all gasp all groan all go with the gavel, all fall as the dancers departed and the chandeliers were packed away

and then the Ffornwg flowed at last through the Versailles room and over the staircase and out of the scullery window weeping for what must disappear and can never be again, the Ffornwg come for the chauffeur's gloves and a handkerchief that belonged to the maid with its embroidery of tansy that never dies

the Ffornwg that says

bab ili bab ili

the Ffornwg that says what history can never say

bab ili bab ili

better death it says

better death than

better death

because death is better than

is better than

always better than

shame

and no translator will ever get that wrong who has sipped and seen his face reflected in its stillwater and only then will the Ffornwg that forgets nothing yet forgives its children go chugging back into its dark tandoor.

The Yellow Dust

THE DUST DEVIL CROSSES the highway ten yards ahead, so close I can see into its weird rotisserie of desert grit, feel its sigh as if it knows exactly where it is going as it brushes over the cholla and spins towards the shadows of the peaks. Our van has stopped close by, its air-con overflow leaking a silver pool. Daniel says he had been here as a child, his father using mittened hands on the steering-wheel, mom wrapping wet towels round the kids' heads. Then he touches me, pointing over saltbush to the dunes. Because there is a man, he swears, a figure, hatless, striding on as if he knows exactly where to go, heading for that first immaculate crest and so beating us by half a mile, each step the first there has ever been in that white dirt. But I know only the devil moves, transparent as an X-ray of myself, a wraith that squeezes between the thorns and will never be left behind.

Acknowledgements

Many thanks to the editors of the following publications in which earlier versions of parts of *To Babel and Back* first appeared: *Amsterdam Review; The London Magazine; Manhattan Review; New Welsh Review; Planet; Poetry Wales; Images of the Valleys* (Inbooks).

A version of 'Paradise Park' appeared in *Paradise Park* (Seren).

I am grateful to the British Council, Welsh Arts Council/Arts Council of Wales, Welsh Books Council and Wales Arts International for their support.

With special thanks to: Beatrice Boctor; Daniel Robicheau; Nazaar Jassim Noori.

Author Note

Robert Minhinnick is an acclaimed author and the editor of *Poetry Wales* magazine. He was born and brought up in south Wales, lives near the sea in Porthcawl, and has read his work around the world from the Amazon to Saskatoon, Helsinki to Baghdad. He won the Forward Prize for his poetry and the Wales Book of the Year for his essays. A freelance writer, he also works for the environmental organisation Sustainable Wales.